Creating Charismatic Bonds in Argentina

Diálogos Series

KRIS LANE, SERIES EDITOR

Understanding Latin America demands dialogue, deep exploration, and frank discussion of key topics. Founded by Lyman L. Johnson in 1992 and edited since 2013 by Kris Lane, the Diálogos Series focuses on innovative scholarship in Latin American history and related fields. The series, the most successful of its type, includes specialist works accessible to a wide readership and a variety of thematic titles, all ideally suited for classroom adoption by university and college teachers.

Also available in the Diálogos Series:

Gendered Crossings: Women and Migration in the Spanish Empire
by Allyson M. Poska
From Shipmates to Soldiers: Emerging Black Identities in the Río de la Plata
by Alex Borucki
Women Drug Traffickers: Mules, Bosses, and Organized Crime by Elaine Carey
Searching for Madre Matiana: Prophecy and Popular Culture in Modern Mexico
by Edward Wright-Rios
Africans into Creoles: Slavery, Ethnicity, and Identity in Colonial Costa Rica
by Russell Lohse
Native Brazil: Beyond the Convert and the Cannibal, 1500–1900
edited by Hal Langfur
Emotions and Daily Life in Colonial Mexico
edited by Javier Villa-Flores and Sonya Lipsett-Rivera
The Course of Andean History by Peter V. N. Henderson
Masculinity and Sexuality in Modern Mexico
edited by Anne Rubenstein and Víctor M. Macías-González
A History of Mining in Latin America: From the Colonial Era to the Present
by Kendall Brown

For additional titles in the Diálogos Series, please visit unmpress.com.

Creating Charismatic Bonds in Argentina

LETTERS TO JUAN AND EVA PERÓN

Donna J. Guy

University of New Mexico Press ～ Albuquerque

Library of Congress Cataloging-in-Publication Data
Names: Guy, Donna J.
Title: Creating charismatic bonds in Argentina : letters to Juan and Eva Perón /
Donna J. Guy.
Description: Albuquerque : University of New Mexico Press, 2016. | Series: Diálogos Series |
Includes bibliographical references and index.
Identifiers: LCCN 2015029047 | ISBN 9780826338372 (cloth : alkaline paper) |
ISBN 9780826338389 (paperback : alkaline paper) | ISBN 9780826338396 (electronic)
Subjects: LCSH: Argentina—Politics and government—1943–1955. | Perón, Juan Domingo,
1895–1974—Correspondence. | Perón, Eva, 1919–1952—Correspondence. | Presidents—
Argentina—Correspondence. | Presidents' spouses—Argentina—Correspondence. | Charisma
(Personality trait)—Political aspects—Argentina—History—20th century. | Letter writing—
Political aspects—Argentina—History—20th century. | Political culture—Argentina—
History—20th century. | Political planning—Argentina—History—20th century.
Classification: LCC F2849.G88 2016 | DDC 320.9820904—dc23
LC record available at http://lccn.loc.gov/2015029047

Cover illustration from *El Alma tutelar para primer grado superior de la escuela primaria*
by Blanca Alicia Casas
Designed by Felicia Cedillos
Composed in Minion 10.25/14
Display fonts are Jenna Sue and ITC New Baskerville

CONTENTS

Acknowledgments   vii

INTRODUCTION
Letter Writing and the Construction of Peronist Charisma   1

CHAPTER 1
Early Correspondence and Eva's Creation of Charismatic Bonds   13

CHAPTER 2
Pensions for the Elderly and Infirm   41

CHAPTER 3
Pent-up Needs
Juan's Plan de Gobierno   67

CHAPTER 4
Reaffirming the Charismatic Bond
The Segundo Plan Quinquenal   85

CHAPTER 5
Children and *la Patria*   107

CHAPTER 6
Charismatic Bonds
How Long Can They Last?   129

CONCLUSION
Reflections on the Enduring Nature of Peronist Charisma   143

Notes   147
Bibliography   161
Index   167

ACKNOWLEDGMENTS

I would like to thank many people who have been involved in this project, although I take personal responsibility for content and accuracy. Gary Hearn photographed archival collections at the national archives. He has also faithfully supported all of my endeavors. Susan Deeds helped copyedit the preliminary and penultimate versions, and Steven Hyland and Stephanie Mitchell commented on the second. I also want to thank Dora Barrancos, Marta Goldberg, Carolina Barry, Adriana Valobra, Ana María Presta, José Luis Moreno, Ricardo Salvatore and his wife, Laura, the staff at the Archivo General de la Nación and its Archivo Intermedio—especially Elizabeth Cipolleta—the staff at the Archivo Consejo Nacional de la Niñez, Adolescencia y la Familia, and the researchers who helped transcribe files. I would also like to thank Dra. Noemí Girbal de Blacha for her help with Ianantuoini, El Segundo Plan Quinquenal. Graciela Braccio also did research for this project. Daniel Eduardo Martínez prepared the graphs of demographic pyramids and migration flow. I would like to thank Lic. Gabriel D. Taruseli for his help securing a scan of Decree 17.252. Osvaldo Barreneche, Juan Barreneche, and Luciana Marangone helped me with archival research after my allergies made it impossible to return. Stephanie Mitchell read later versions of the manuscripts. I owe a great debt to my allergist, Dr. Martin Bartels, for controlling my allergic response to old papers for many years, as well as to Dr. Eduardo Moon who cared for me in Argentina as a friend and as a physician. I also want to than Kris Lane and Clark Whitehorn for their help and support.

Letter Writing and the Construction of Peronist Charisma

POPULIST, CHARISMATIC LEADERS have been exceedingly difficult to study from an unbiased perspective. Very often presidential history in Latin America gets written according to traditional party-oriented histories. The authors of such histories might verify their views by claiming that they know how "the people" felt about the leaders. Both Juan Perón and Eva Duarte de Perón, Argentine president (1946–1955, 1973–1974) and First Lady (1946–1952), have been described as charismatic, populist politicians, but they are often studied individually rather than as a couple whose close emotional bonds with the people fortified their political power. This book focuses on the first era of Peronism, from 1946 to 1955, when, up until 1952, both the president and the First Lady used charismatic methods to link themselves to Argentine supporters through letter writing. It situates the people—rural dwellers and internal migrants as opposed to organized workers or politicians—and their efforts to reach Juan and Eva to shape the direction of their policies. In this way poor Argentines accepted a charismatic bond, one that consisted of personal relationships conditioned by a number of political, economic, and social factors.[1]

Charisma is a slippery concept that describes intensely personal emotional connections between a leader and his or her followers. While some writers have attempted to root this attraction in the nature of the political, religious, or social position of a historical actor, others have focused on the individual's age, physical attributes, spirituality, or physical suffering. Often the followers

in this charismatic process are defined as irrational, overly emotional, or igno-
rant. This places all the responsibility in the hands of the powerful person,
rather than asking how the less powerful could help shape, and even profit
from, the development of an attractive and caring personality in a leader.[2]

This book considers hundreds of letters (once presumed burned) to Juan
and Eva from their people as well as correspondence solicited by Juan. It
promotes a view that charismatic bonds in Argentina have been formed as
much by Argentines as by their leaders, and it demonstrates how letter writing at that time instilled a sense of nationalism and unity, particularly during
the first five-year plan initiated in 1946. It goes beyond the question of how
charisma influenced elections and class affiliation to address broader impli-
cations. Implicitly it offers a new methodology to study the formation of
charisma in literate countries where not only propaganda and public media
but also private correspondence defined and helped shape political policies.

These letters also resonate when studied from new perspectives on
nineteenth-century Argentine caudillos. Ariel de la Fuente has argued that
caudillismo should be seen "as a reciprocal relationship between leaders
and followers . . . who projected their own values onto the strongman."[3]
Within one hundred years, however, this relationship had modernized, and
people had much more to say than merely extolling their leader or asking
for food rations, as Ricardo Salvatore has shown for the period under Juan
Manuel de Rosas.[4]

Thus, this book is also an effort to show how correspondence from the
people, particularly the poor, demonstrates patterns of continuity that link
Peronism to earlier political parties and institutions that also promoted
charity, philanthropy, and responses to individual needs. Eva did not invent
the welfare state, but she found new ways to implement support previously
supplied by private organizations. What Juan invented, however, was the
invitation to every citizen to make suggestions for economic and social policies for a five-year plan.

Five-year plans, first introduced in Stalinist Russia in 1928, proved attractive to some socialist, communist, democratic, and populist governments
that sought a national planning model, but Juan's populist call for all to send
in suggestions was unique—although, as we shall see later, citizens' suggestions became important only in the second five-year plan.

While this has rarely been replicated in other societies, Juan initially viewed the implementation of the two plans as an impersonal one. People wrote to Juan, but he showed little willingness to engage in personal contact with citizens. Instead, he preferred to promote a welfare state through the bureaucratic processing of letters. For these reasons it becomes important to study the formation of charismatic bonds with both Juan and Eva to show how their combined styles created a comprehensive approach to poor people. Eva's hands-on style helped diminish the visibility of the welfare state, while Juan worked to expand state welfare programs.

The letters also highlight the needs of the very poor, often elderly people living outside the province of Buenos Aires. Their entreaties and responses by Juan and Eva add to our understanding of how nonunionized working-class people became part of the Peronist world of charisma and how their suffering shaped national policy. Their letters show us how Peronism was experienced in the interior, where people made suggestions not only for themselves but also for others.

Early studies of Peronist charisma traced its origins to three possibilities: the willingness of an authoritarian and populist leader to use his or her personality and political bargaining power to obtain the political and emotional support of presumably illiterate masses, particularly the rural migrants who flooded the capital city of Buenos Aires in the 1930s and '40s; the willingness of immigrant and second-generation workers of immigrant parentage to ally themselves with Peronism rather than socialism; and the ability of Eva to promote an emotional charismatic relationship with the people, especially with women, by being a "bridge of love" between the workers and Juan. Most of these studies focus on charisma and its role in the formation of political allegiances and its impact on the 1946 presidential elections. They also assume that many of the internal migrants were male and politically inexperienced, much like the rest of those who chose not to migrate.[5]

To understand these letters and what role they may have played in the development of charismatic personalities and their impact on political, economic, and social policies in Argentina, we must examine the early biographical accounts of Juan and Eva. During their lifetimes, a series of books—mostly critical of Peronism and its leaders—began to appear. In 1953 George Blanksten, a Washington insider and professor of political science, published *Perón's Argentina*, in which he generally criticizes both Juan and Eva for their demagogic activities. He admits that most US observers believed that Perón had few supporters among the working class but many within the military. Yet, as he himself writes, "Some case may be made for drawing a curious negative correlation between the 'North American' experts and Argentine political observers: as the former become more convinced that Perón is unpopular, among Argentines, the latter retreat from this view."[6] Nevertheless, his book frequently quotes unflattering myths and commentary from a *Time* magazine report on the coup. When he explains the workers' support, he argues that if Perón "were to bid for the votes and the support of the workers, their political action must be cast in terms of *personalismo*— loyalty to a particular politician, Perón, rather than formulation by labor of its own political and economic objectives."[7] Similarly, his chapter on Eva portrays her as a strong and caring leader who gave aid, comfort, and the vote to women but insisted on strict loyalty from them to her husband, even though recent studies show that the women in her Peronist Women's Political Party (Partido Peronista Femenino) took strict orders from her, not her husband.[8] The early biographies demonstrate that leaders, not rank and file, defined the relationship of the Peronists to the people, and these biographies define the relationship between Juan and his wife as a traditional, hierarchical one where Eva simply followed Juan's orders. The fact that Eva had written *La razón de mi vida*, an autobiography that reifies the president while embodying Eva as a loyal wife and comrade, did little to dispel traditional notions of Eva.[9]

María Main, writing as Fleur Cowles and no friend of the Peróns, attributes Eva's connections to the people to her radio program. This perspective—that Eva organized Juan's supporters—has again appeared in more recent studies of Peronism. Yet Main admits that after meeting Juan during a fundraiser to support victims of the 1944 San Juan earthquake, Eva "started a daily program in which she dramatically acted out an account of Perón's welfare ideas and objectives. . . . Evita explained to her listeners just how Colonel Perón disposed of every case. She obtained records from his deputies and office secretaries and brought the story of the 'handsome colonel's good deeds,' wondrously romanticized to the masses."[10] By the end of the book, Juan and Eva are compared to the nineteenth-century dictator Rosas and his wife, doña Encarnación. Main has no idea how, for example, illiterate women, often widows, made their mark on requests for subsidies, nor how others successfully made demands for help from the president and First Lady.

Others, like María Flores, attribute to Eva the ability to organize the workers' protest that led to Juan's return to freedom on October 17, 1945, after military officials had sent him to political prison for becoming too powerful. She incorrectly gives Eva the credit for closing down the principal government-subsidized charity, the Society of Beneficence (Sociedad de Beneficencia), in 1946 because wealthy elite women ran the many orphanages and hospitals. She also repeats accusations of anti-Peronists that Juan and Eva had millions of dollars in foreign bank accounts—something never verified.[11]

In addition, Flores questions Eva's religiosity. "*Peronismo* was a religion and she repeatedly declared herself as its fanatical devotee. There is no doubt that if she had dared she would have set about disestablishing the Roman Catholic Church in Argentina."[12] Flores's evidence for this view was the fact that both Juan and Eva believed in Spiritism. Eva's confessor, Father Benítez, forgave her (especially since she claimed to have received visits from General José de San Martín, known as the Liberator of South America, who is buried in the Buenos Aires cathedral), but the Vatican did not approve of such beliefs. These letters show the fervent Catholicism practiced in Argentina at the time, as well as how people appealed to Eva through religious metaphors, but they reveal no evidence of Spiritism.[13]

Generally speaking, early accounts of Juan and Eva were rooted in political and partisan history and often recounted many of the negative myths about both of them. Eva became portrayed as a prostitute and Juan as a fascist, particularly after the publication of the *Argentine Blue Book* in 1946. This pamphlet—produced under the direction of Spruille Braden, US ambassador to Argentina—urged Argentines not to vote for Juan in the 1946 elections. Braden accused Juan of being a fascist and trying to disrupt politics in the Americas. In turn, Juan used the publication as a referendum for Argentines to vote either for "Braden ó Perón" and to reject US influence on Argentine elections, ultimately winning in one of the freest elections in Argentine history.[14]

The classic biographers of Juan and Eva did not have access to the cache of letters that are now available, nor did they focus on popular culture, including music. Furthermore, they focused on just one or the other of the two leaders. Maryssa Navarro and Nicholas Fraser's *Eva Perón* benefited from a wide variety of contemporary oral interviews from people who knew her well, and it remains a classic. Another iconic study of Eva, Julie M. Taylor's *Eva Perón: Myths of a Woman*, also utilized extensive oral interviews with distinct groups of Argentines in an effort to sort out the class basis of myths about Eva. Joseph A. Page's biography of Juan relied more on printed records. Together, the three constitute the foundational biographies of Juan and Eva. More recently, in 2002 Mariano Ben Plotkin published *Mañana es San Perón*, an excellent study of the institutional mechanisms used to inculcate loyalty and devotion to the Peróns that has also become a classic. He utilized documents from the Eva Perón Foundation that had been unavailable to earlier authors. Not directed at replacing the earlier studies, my book does not intend to challenge these works but rather to provide access to new documents that often represent the recently recovered voices of other groups.[15]

For years, people tried to unravel the complex charismatic relationships between Juan, Eva, and the Argentine public. Originally fascism and authoritarianism provided the explanation for Juan's hold over his military followers, and evidence of this appears in the correspondence, not so much on the part of the president but rather from his followers. Then in 1984 the eminent US historian Robert Potash published a series of documents regarding the secret group that planned the 1943 coup and proved that Juan was not only a central conspirator at that time, he held power to maintain the loyalty of the other coup members through their unsigned, undated letters of resignation. Potash's book portrays Perón not as a fascist but as a very clever politician who could control allies, regardless of their ideology, through fear of resignation. In terms of his charismatic relationship with the military, fear thus played an important part.[16]

Sorting out Perón's relationship with laborers proved to be more difficult due to the contemporary phenomenon of internal migration from interior provinces to Buenos Aires. Initially, historians like Samuel Baily posited that relatively unsophisticated male migrant workers looked to Perón, much as they would have followed a labor boss or someone with whom they had a patron-client relationship. Baily was soon criticized by Juan Corradi, who notes that "to interpret Perón's appeal as exclusively charismatic, that is, as the irrational attachment of undereducated, unorganized masses of migrants from the countryside to a Latin *caudillo*, is to forget the important role played by older, mature worker organizations," implying that the more educated workers did not enjoy a charismatic relationship with Juan, because such workers were more rational.[17] More recent works, such as those by Daniel James and James Brennan, have reinforced this anticharismatic labor movement theory.

In a 2004 article sociologist Daniela di Piramo argues for a more fluid interpretation of Peronist charisma. "The relation between agency and structure or between the charismatic leader and the systems that constitute society is shown to be interactive, fluid and immediate, accompanied by the destruction and reconstruction of institutions in the rational pursuit of a new social order."[18] She further defines a series of strategies manipulated to reaffirm Peronist legitimacy. The first involves material benefits that Perón offered his followers. The second, a discursive strategy, articulates values and goals that include "moments of nationalistic sentiment, quasi-religious connotations that hail the leader as the as 'the savior' . . . and the offering to the followers of a sense of political identity and purpose." The last strategy enshrines Peronism through "rituals and symbolic associations that shape national culture and mythology." Once again, the transmission of these strategies flows downward from above.[19]

Douglas Madsen and Peter G. Snow take a somewhat different approach by examining the political phenomenon of Peronism based upon theories of charisma and political surveys. They define charisma as an asymmetrical relationship between the leader and the followers, one marked by great passion. This relationship usually occurs during a time of crisis or transition, a phenomenon that facilitates what they call the "charismatic bond," that is, the two-way relationship between the ruler and the ruled. The charismatic bond, they suggest, could refashion charisma, something Max Weber considered short-lived, into a longer-lasting phenomenon. While they present an intriguing hypothesis, when they try to analyze the surveys their apparent lack of understanding of gender relations makes it hard for them to understand why Argentine women acted differently from Argentine men in their perceptions of the Peronist charismatic bond. Their analysis simply excludes gender as a category even though the differences between women and men were notable.[20] And, although they do not mention it, after Peronists enacted female suffrage in 1947, electoral results indicated that the social basis of Peronism changed and became more linked to women and the popular classes than it was in 1946.

Recently, new studies have emphasized the role of movies and radio as factors in the rise of both popular culture and the bonds forged by Juan and Eva. Oscar Chamosa explored the relationship of the 1943 military coup that brought Juan to power with the desire to "instill the moral values allegedly ingrained in rural criollo folklore" through the sponsorship of folk music on the radio as well as movies dealing with this subject. Commercial folk music expanded considerably under Peronism, while the urban tango was censored by removing lyrics that questioned the social mobility of the working class. In its place, according to Matthew B. Karush, more orchestral versions prospered.[21]

Karush also contends that Juan relied on the morality model of the evolving Argentine cinema to phrase social mobility in a group context: "The language with which Perón appealed so powerfully to workers was essentially melodramatic; in its Manichean moralism, its attack on the greed and selfishness of the rich, and its tendency to depict the poor as the authentic Argentine pueblo, it bore the unmistakable traces of the movies, music, and radio programs of the 1930s."[22] And, despite the belief that all workers benefited from Peronism, this model also foments ideas of personal desire to consume, which shows up in the letters people wrote to Juan and Eva.[23] These cultural mechanisms also helped cement charismatic ties between the people and the president and his wife. The letters referred to in this book reaffirm the significance of the melodramatic, but they also emphasize how the Peróns were forced to confront the melodramas of the poor on an individual basis, not just a group one, in order to win their allegiance.

Until now, proving these cultural and emotional ties has been difficult because scholars labored under the mistaken belief that all letters written to Juan and Eva were destroyed by the military in 1955. Even if this had been true, public burnings could never completely erase traces of these letters, because many people hid artifacts related to Juan and Eva, some of which have become commodities on the Internet. Radio- and cinema-focused magazines also helped preserve this evidence. In the past decade several treasure troves of letters in public archives have become available for consultation. Some of them were in public repositories but remained hidden from easy access by the organizational structure of institutions like the Argentine National Archive (Archivo General de la Nación Argentina). Others have only recently been catalogued and made accessible to researchers. The archive of the Argentine National Council on the Child, Adolescent and Family (ACNNAF), no longer open to researchers, contains fifty thousand files on children who entered the Society of Beneficence, Defenders of Minors, and juvenile reformatories between 1880 and 1955. Some of these letters include correspondence to Juan and Eva. Provincial archives evidently also have letters. The task of understanding them and the role they may have played in the development of charismatic personalities has only begun to be explored. The results challenge our preconceptions of how Peronism functioned.

A 1966 compilation of Peronist popular poetry and songs written to or about Juan and Eva Perón, rarely consulted by historians, serves as an early indicator of how melodrama, the tango, and folk music became venues for interactions between Juan, Eva, and the masses. Collected by Julio Darío Alessandro with help from the publishers Grupo Editor de Buenos Aires, the poems document charismatic relationships in newspapers, labor union publications, and poetry anthologies. The book includes tangos written by famous composers and lyricists as well as many unknown authors who supported the Peronist government.[24]

The official Peronist view of melodrama was that under the guidance of Juan and Eva the plight of the poor no longer existed. An anonymous tango entitled "Milonga descamisada" described the difference between the tangos of the past and those under Peronism. "It isn't the plaintive song of painful tears, but the voice of a working-class (*compañera*) girl who shimmers with the guitar." The boy in the song is not an upper-class dandy, but a happy man (*el varón alegre*), and in the countryside the Peronist tango is as blue as the sky. In other words, working-class people no longer lamented but rather celebrated their lives through the Peronist tango. A different story emerges from the contemporary letters and petitions.[25]

Another example of Peronism and popular culture comes from a famous tango lyricist, Homero Manzi. He wrote "Songs of a Minstrel to Sra. Eva Perón" (Versos de un payador a la señora Eva Perón) and told the story of a wandering minstrel who arrived at Eva's door and compared Juan to Eva. The song served as a bridge between the two dominant forms of national public music, the rural folk song and the urban tango.

He [Perón] is the tip of the lance and you are the point of love;
He is the cry of honor that reaches us
And you are the domesticating hand that eliminates pain.
He is the great sower and you are hope.[26]

These patently sexual lyrics show the great faith that people in the countryside placed in the success of both Juan and Eva, just as these people believed their crops to be their salvation.

Most people who simply sent letters, petitions, and suggestions were literate. The few who were not used others to record their thoughts and then signed with a thumbprint. Schooling among the poor and rural folk often amounted only to a type of functional literacy that enabled people to read signs and newspapers and to sign their names. Very few went beyond the third grade. Yet the high degree of minimal literacy, especially among older adults and youngsters who had to help support their families, produced many requests for construction of more rural schools and trade schools for older as well as younger people. Some parents pleaded with Juan and Eva to enroll their children in free boarding schools, thereby challenging the efficacy of public schools for the poor who could not afford to clothe and feed their offspring. These petitioners living in the interior joined the ranks of enthusiastic urban supporters of Peronism in Buenos Aires. Thus the idea that Peronists were only people with little education who migrated from the interior to Buenos Aires was a class-based fiction rather than fact. Indeed, most of the illiterate and the poor stayed at home for a variety of reasons, often related to illness, age, or poverty.

Before 1946, organized charity was both state subsidized and funded by religious, professional, and immigrant groups. In Buenos Aires, the Society of Beneficence received funds from the National Lottery to run hospitals and orphanages. Elite families donated large sums of money, and orphans went out on the street to collect contributions during annual drives for the society as well as for other philanthropies. People traditionally wrote letters to the head of the society asking for alms and invoking kindness to the poor and suffering as a basic duty of the organization. Prizes, such as the cash awarded for the most virtuous (Premio a la Virtud), often went to those, usually widows, who had the most sorrowful story. While the province of Buenos Aires always had funds for the poor, as did the city of Buenos Aires, the least privileged in the provinces relied on letters sent to Buenos Aires and to Catholic and immigrant charities. By the 1930s, religious and immigrant charity proved to be insufficient and prompted many desperate men and women to seek better jobs and more help in Buenos Aires.

Under Peronism, those who went to Buenos Aires, especially working mothers and their children, could stay in residences founded by Eva and shop in grocery stores established by her foundation. The orphanages and hospitals run by the society were eventually folded into the national welfare system. Those who stayed in the provinces benefited from the expansion of poor pensions originally distributed by the Society of Beneficence to urban poor in Buenos Aires. Just as he began to close down the Society of Benefi-cence, Juan Perón enacted new laws regarding such pensions in 1946. The new ones actually favored the rural poor over his traditional urban clientele by making it necessary for local authorities to vouch for the poverty or illness of the petitioners. People created their own charismatic bridges to welfare by writing directly to the president and First Lady rather than to the bureau-cratic agency that replaced the Society of Beneficence. Symbolically, Juan eventually turned over the process to his wife Eva, as seen in chapter 2. He clearly intended to use the benefits to slow down migration to the cities, while Eva simultaneously worked to set up temporary shelters for the fami-lies that arrived in Buenos Aires bereft of safety and familial networks, as seen in chapter 1.

Collections of letters from the people to Juan and Eva demonstrate dis-tinctive uses of correspondence to promote the desires not only of the leaders but also the followers. Furthermore, many of these people proved to be quite effective at soliciting favors at various times. Such successes point to the inti-macy of letter writing as a way to promote a fictive connection between the masses and the Peronist leaders, something that would have been impossible if there had been high rates of illiteracy. They also reveal that the letter writ-ers had clearly formulated goals, some of which fit with Juan and Eva's plans, and others that simply did not. Nevertheless, while Argentines showed humility and deference to national leaders, they had no problems expressing their own ideas. Some letters provoked personal interventions on the part of the president or the First Lady. Other ideas actually became incorporated into Peronist programs.

This book is divided into six chapters. Chapter 1 tells the early stories of people who wrote letters to Juan (at his invitation) and to Eva (unsolicited) seeking housing for migrants relocating to the national capital and making personal entreaties to the couple. Chapter 2 explores unsolicited letters for pensions for the poor and infirm previously granted by the Society of Benef-icence. Chapters 3 and 4 deal with Juan's effort to get suggestions regarding his first and second five-year plans, and chapter 5 explores unsolicited letters from people seeking help for their children, basing their petitions on notions of *la patria* (the nation). Chapter 6 recounts the impact of Eva's death, the inability of Peronism to address many personal problems, and how such failures might represent a rupture in the charismatic bond for some. The letters represent a sampling because many files are incomplete. In addition, some people wrote to make suggestions for the five-year plans and to request subsidies without referring directly to the Peróns.

CHAPTER I

Early Correspondence and Eva's Creation of Charismatic Bonds

LETTER WRITING HAS forged bonds of communication between political leaders and members of the Latin American public for hundreds of years. During the colonial period not only elites but also educated Indians and mestizos (people of Indian-Spanish heritage) and *mulatos* (people of African and Spanish heritage) wrote to Spanish officials to plead for help or to criticize colonial policies. Even if people were illiterate, scribes or notary publics provided the literacy necessary for petitions. Indeed, the bureaucratic nature of the Spanish Empire required the existence of literate individuals who served as go-betweens for a generally illiterate public and a literate bureaucracy.[1]

In Argentina literacy became important in urban areas where commerce, religion, and empire formed the basis of economic relations. Religious institutions and private tutors taught young people to read and write until public schools opened shortly after Argentina's independence from Spain in 1810. Domingo Sarmiento, one of the first presidents of a united Argentina (which had been divided into the port area and interior during civil wars in the first half of the nineteenth century), became devoted to public education. Although self-taught, Sarmiento worked to promote literacy and public education even before becoming president in 1868. As head of state, he expanded the number of government-supported schools. His successor to the presidency, Nicolás Avellaneda (1874–1880), had served as his minister of education. This sustained commitment to public education enabled common people to write petitions and letters. Whether they used notary publics or wrote their own missives, widows, soldiers, and charitable groups increasingly and regularly petitioned the president and congress for financial support to carry out their endeavors.[2]

Hipólito Yrigoyen (1916–1922, 1928–1930) became the most visible president before Juan Perón to encourage the poor to ask him for aid. Much like Eva Perón, Yrigoyen became known for his philanthropy, his willingness to meet citizens, and his compassion during his first administration. In fact he proudly acknowledged that he donated his salary to the publicly subsidized Society of Beneficence (Sociedad de Beneficencia) and permitted people to approach him for charity. An interesting letter from the archives of the Society of Beneficence reveals that Yrigoyen's reputation for generosity led a young man, orphaned since the age of two months, to send a letter to the society in 1928 asking the group to intercede in his efforts to obtain an interview with Yrigoyen. He also wanted to find out his parents' identity, but he obtained neither. We can surmise that this young man probably was neither the first nor the last to write to Yrigoyen. During his second campaign for the presidency, Yrigoyen had a propaganda film made in 1928 that extolled the philanthropic accomplishments of his political party, the Radicals. One might argue that Yrigoyen set a model of beneficence that also provided a way to bypass, rather than support, the society that had become a symbol of elite charity by the 1940s. He also did this by receiving petitioners at his home.[3]

Perón ascended to power through a military coup in 1943. By then Argentine citizens, both rural and urban, had long-standing needs, many of which were ultimately addressed by Juan and Eva. For countries involved in World War II, consumer demands had taken second place to the war effort. In Argentina, a desire for a better life resulted from other factors. The impact of declining world prices for grains and beef during the Depression, increased migration of poor Argentines to Buenos Aires in search of work, and the toll that these events placed on families and communities became a crisis by the 1940s. Not only did migrants see the difference between the way they had lived in the countryside compared to the better standards of living promised to organized urban workers by Perón, those who remained at home found themselves bereft of family and community support and unable to enjoy consumer benefits offered by the new democratic government. High postwar inflation rates did not help. Provincial governments had little to offer those left on the farms and ranches, while migrants turned to new sources of beneficence coming from Eva and her transit homes (homeless shelters, described below) and from Perón's government.[4]

Immigrant communities needed personal friends with power, too. Between 1880 and 1914, hundreds of thousands of immigrants landed in Argentina, mostly settling initially in the city and province of Buenos Aires, as well as Santa Fe, Mendoza, and other provinces.[5] Many lived modestly at best and by the 1940s confronted new realities both in Europe and in Argentina. They found themselves part of the aging population and often ill. Although few became citizens, immigrants could receive all social welfare services. Furthermore, their children born in Argentina automatically became citizens and part of the Argentine system; politicians ignored them at their risk. Thus it is no surprise, for example, that Perón went out of his way to court the Jewish community by making Argentina the first Latin American country to recognize the State of Israel in 1948 and by forming a community group to oppose the Anti-Peronist Jews. Indeed, Perón periodically met with different immigrant groups to gain their support, something that had not occurred since Marcelo T. de Alvear's presidency (1922–1928). At the same time he retained strong support among many military men who had participated in the 1943 military coup, as well as among labor unions.[6]

Since independence, two Argentine realities existed. One, the most visible, included urban areas of the coastal region. The other comprised the interior where residents suffered from a shortage of reasonable housing, economic activities, and schools. Crop failures, changing prices for beef, and family disintegration increasingly led to population declines. The residents of coastal urban polities assiduously ignored rural areas and small towns of the Argentine countryside to promote lower food prices for Buenos Aires. *Porteños* had their own problems. The arrival of immigrants and then of new, mostly poor internal migrants led to the creation of many shantytowns and new political demands by urban dwellers. Under these circumstances, urban and rural people all sought a personal and emotive connection with the president, as well as solutions to perceived problems. This dichotomy changed urban landscapes and resulted in a steady migration to the capital city by people in search of jobs and succor while the provinces suffered. Migrants and those staying at home all needed to believe in a knight in shining armor.

Equally important, between 1936 and 1946 a silent but visible female

demographic revolution took place in the capital city of Buenos Aires. It is
this constituency of women, as well as children, that became the focus of
Eva's attentions. While historians have no national censuses to track population movements between 1914 and this period, the 1936 Buenos Aires census
and the abbreviated 1946 fourth national census conducted a decade later,
just as the first Peronist government took power, provided clear evidence of
a massive demographic change. The censuses showed that while Argentina
had always been viewed as a land of immigrants, mostly men, adult foreign
immigration in the 1930s and 1940s had exercised little impact on the porteño
population under the age of forty. The opposite was true in the case of female
internal migration to the national capital. Women and their children, often
needy, dotted the urban landscape.

    While internal migration also occurred in provincial capital cities, the
national capital proved to be particularly sensitive to this Argentine demographic shift. It was home to the port through which new immigrants arrived
and the key destination for the greater number of internal migrants. Male
immigrants had buoyed the masculinity rate to 116 percent in 1895 (that is,
116 males for 100 females). After 1914, however, many fewer immigrants, either

CHART 1. 1936 and 1947 Buenos Aires Male and Female Migration Comparisons

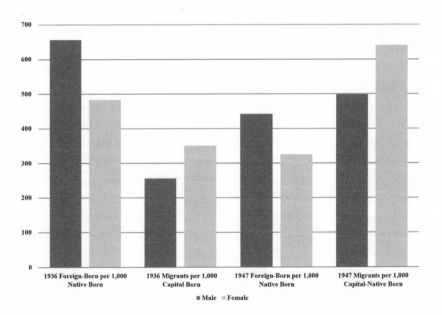

CHART 2. 1947 Buenos Aires, Males and Females

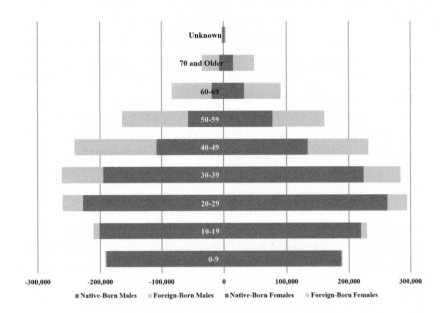

Native-Born Males · Foreign-Born Males · Native-Born Females · Foreign-Born Females

CHART 3. 1936 Buenos Aires, Males and Females

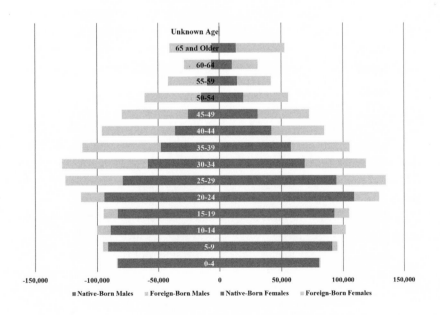

Native-Born Males · Foreign-Born Males · Native-Born Females · Foreign-Born Females

male or female, stayed there, and the masculinity rate decreased to 99.3 percent
in 1936 and 94.5 percent in 1947. These numbers, according to census takers,
 mirrored the situation in the United States and other countries that had
absorbed the massive prewar immigration movements. However, casualties of
war and increased war work in factories could not explain Argentina's
increased numbers of females in the capital city. The total number of female
migrants of all ages almost doubled in Buenos Aires, from 214,556 in 1936 to
396,560 in 1947, despite migratory ebbs and flows. The 1947 population pyramid
reflected both those who returned to the countryside, the new migrants, and
the expansion of the female population. Women, especially after the rise of Eva
Perón, became a principal political target for the new Peronist movement, and
this reality encouraged plans for female suffrage.[7]

By the 1940s old social safety nets no longer proved useful, and migrants
eventually turned to the new world of Peronist politics. Meanwhile, immigrants who were not citizens grew older and more dependent upon public
welfare facilities. They, along with urban folks not employed in labor unions,
turned to the president and his wife because they had problems that could
not be resolved by other means. Letters became the medium of communication, in addition to personal meetings with the needy.

This chapter focuses on how Eva Perón's activities responded to these
demographic and economic realities. Beginning with the public's exposure
to Eva as a radio and movie star before she met Juan, it explores the various
mechanisms she used to respond to the public's need for charismatic bonds.
She did not do this by closing the elite Society of Beneficence, but rather by
creating new sources of public access to the president's wife. The chapter also
introduces the voice of the poor.

The Public's Discovery of Eva

How did people come to know about Eva? They already knew about her as
the star of several radio programs since 1939. She also had some movie parts
and appeared regularly in magazines for devotees of radio soap operas and
the cinema. So before she met Juan, she had a flourishing career with the help
of her brother, Juan Duarte.[8] While she earned very little, increasingly people recognized her. She became the first president of the newly organized
labor union for performers in the broadcasting industry. She thrilled

audiences, mostly females, with her enactments of famous women in history. After Juan met Eva in 1944, the young radio actress was quickly drawn to politics as well as to the dashing military man. Shortly thereafter, on a program entitled "The Soldier's Revolution will be the Revolution of the Argentine People," Eva and her script emphasized the ways that the 1943 military coup had helped people's lives. She commented, "There was a man who could bring dignity to the notion of work, a soldier of the people who could feel the flame of social justice. . . . it was he who decisively helped the people's Revolution."[9] Then Juan gave a talk penned by Eva's scriptwriter. Here is clear evidence that Eva's profession served as a training ground for the increasingly popular Juan. While his military experience taught him hierarchy and bureaucracy, Eva taught him the role of communications in the development of charismatic traits.

The first public speech by Eva came from the state radio station on July 25, 1946, and specifically asked the Argentine women who benefited from Perón's campaign to help lower the cost of living. She began by greeting the Argentine women as descendants of those who helped fight for the nation. She went on to identify Perón as the person who would sacrifice everything for the happiness of the people from his position as secretary of labor and welfare. She urged women as wives, mothers, and girlfriends to support those who continued to fight for the people by not fearing to report sellers who raised prices, and not to pay prices higher than those established by the government.[10] This speech showed her early interest in women's issues, but not feminist issues, and her willingness to be a liaison between workers, women, and the future president.

Contemporary accounts note that Eva's working-class background endeared her to the public at the same time that military and political critics were horrified by her lack of style, class, and demeanor. The number of letters to Eva began to soar once Juan became president. According to Navarro and Fraser, the newspaper *La Democracia* claimed that by May 1948 Eva received twelve thousand letters per day from petitioners, prompting her to organize her charities more formally. It is hard to verify the accuracy of this seemingly exaggerated figure, but the method used by the Ministry of Technical Affairs and the Ministry of the Interior eventually numbered the files coming from the presidency and to the Eva Perón Foundation (Fundación Eva Perón), revealing far lower counts.[11]

The nature of the initial letters to Eva emphasized personal difficulties and the belief that Eva would understand the plight of the desperate. Characteristically, these letters included exaggerated salutations to Juan and Eva, as well as flowery and stylized language. Many, if translated verbatim, would appear to be very stilted compositions. Thus, while the salutations remain the same, the body of the petitions in translation reflect more modern language usage. We see this in a letter written by a single mother, a domestic servant hospitalized with diphtheria. This young woman felt compelled to deal with a secret she had never revealed, even to her own family. Thus she took the opportunity to request that Eva arrange for her six-month-old infant to remain in the foundling home, as no one back in her town in the province of Buenos Aires knew about the child. To that end she wrote on October 20, 1947:

> Respectable Lady, first of all please forgive me for daring to write to you but I find myself in a desperate situation . . . and you are my only hope. I am a single mother living in Buenos Aires and my parents don't know that I left the child in the foundling home . . . for six months and in December I will have to retrieve him—that is, in three days. But I don't want to tell my parents and it is for this reason that I write to you. I know that one word from you to this home will persuade them to keep the boy for a while longer until I can take care of him in some other way. I will thank you with all my life and I have great faith in you as I always have in General Perón.[12]

She signed the letter with a name she admitted was not hers, but she gave the first two names of her child and claimed that that the foundling home would be able to identify the boy. She then wrote to the foundling home to tell them that she had already petitioned Eva using a false name. This was a clever move on her part, as the Society of Beneficence was under federal intervention ordered by Juan. As a result, the boy remained in the foundling home. This young mother probably was not the first to utilize connections with Eva for her own benefit and would not be the last, as requests continued to pour in. In many ways this two-way relationship between the masses and the Peróns could be both useful and problematic for all concerned. This young child, never reclaimed by his mother, was eventually adopted to protect his mother from having to reveal her sexual indiscretions to her parents.

Legally recognized by 1948, Eva's foundation had moved from the Secretariat of Labor to its own lodgings in what is currently the University of Buenos Aires Faculty of Engineering on Paseo Colón in downtown Buenos Aires. There she reputedly spent many hours meeting face-to-face with those people fortunate enough to get in to see her. She listened to people's problems and handed out goods, services, and even homes.

Beyond asking for jobs or complaining about government, Argentines from all walks of life, both rich and poor—but more often the poor—sent letters to Juan and Eva Perón and went to see them looking for material, medical, educational, and social improvements. Juan was more difficult to reach, and almost all letters requesting appointments to see him went unanswered—or the petitioners were asked to meet bureaucratic officials—until Eva's death in July 1952. Eva was more accessible. According to Nestor Ferioli, and based upon Eva's autobiography, *La razón de mi vida*, Argentines began writing her letters as soon as Juan took office, and crowds of poor people began to form lines in front of the presidential residence to seek help. By January 1947, with Eva's help, some twenty-five families received new homes. Ferioli also noted that Eva started the tradition of giving out cider, a traditional drink at Christmas. These descriptions of Eva's formative activism are difficult to affirm because so many letters were destroyed during the 1955 military coup.[13] In the early accounts, particularly in Peronist newspapers *La Democracia* and *El Laborista*, news of Eva's initial labors to aid the poor certainly publicized her activities. As early as January 1947 *La Democracia* reported Eva's efforts to provide medicine and clothing to textile workers and to distribute government subsidies to the very poor.[14] Following the Latin American tradition in which Catholic parents often select more influential people to serve as godparents, Juan and Eva were frequently asked to perform that duty. Eva also served as symbolic *madrina*, or godmother, to kindergartens as well as to infants. The act of becoming madrina was more compelling than the US tradition of kissing babies.[15]

When Eva went to Europe in June 1947, her trip became the subject of film reels shown in theaters, along with newspaper coverage all over Argentina. The *New York Times* began to follow her after June 9, and on July 14 *Time* magazine even put her picture on its cover.

Shortly after Eva returned an international star, Juan allowed her to take credit for the subsequent passage of female suffrage in Argentina, even though he had promised from the beginning of his administration to honor the 1945 Pan-American Act of Chapultepec that mandated female suffrage in the Americas and had set up his own bureau to promote suffrage.[16]

In another popular gesture, Eva became an intermediary between the importers of antibiotic drugs and the people desperate to receive them. Before Argentina produced its own antibiotics, few people could obtain them. The Peronist newspaper *El Laborista* related a tale to its readers on November 22, 1947. It seems that Elida Nedina de Graf came to the paper to tell how a cousin of hers, a young laborer, had a terrible infection and needed one of these wonder drugs. *El Laborista* contacted National Deputy Rudolfo A. Decker, who then contacted Eva. Eva (or Evita as she was called by the newspaper) answered Decker, telling him that he should obtain the drug for Elida's cousin. The newspaper noted: "Streptomycin, today the medicine of the rich and powerful, has been transformed by the work and grace of this admirable woman." Earlier, labor unions had gathered funds to pay for antibiotics; apparently the newspaper had occasionally used its own funds for this purpose.[17] Eva's actions, in turn, led Domingo Mercante, the governor of the province of Buenos Aires and publisher of the newspaper, to establish a streptomycin committee to ensure fairer distribution of the antibiotic. Eventually, Perón permitted Squibb Laboratories to produce penicillin in Argentina, thereby diminishing the need to make special requests for antibiotics. Later, as we shall see, Eva became the intermediary for people who wanted automobiles, just as she had done with antibiotics.

In late December 1947 Mercante's paper, *El Laborista*, again praised Eva for inviting one hundred poor children from Santiago del Estero province to Buenos Aires. Their arrival prompted a public meeting with many photo opportunities. Aided by a new group of roving social workers, the children had been selected for a free vacation during the First Lady's trip to Santiago. For the next few days the newpaper focused on Eva's interactions with the children. One article demonstrated that social workers could be very useful to identify and analyze the plight of the poor.[18] All these efforts made Eva highly visible to the Argentine public, even before the Eva Perón Foundation began to function in a consistent fashion.

These early experiences related to medicine, along with her friendship with Ramón Carillo, who designed the Peronist public health program, led to the establishment of clinics throughout the Argentine interior and probably formed the origins of the 1951 famed *tren sanitario*, a train that traveled throughout Argentina equipped with the latest medicines, medical specialists, and social workers to attend to the needs of the poor. In the meantime, Eva turned her attention to the plight of women and children who migrated to Buenos Aires and had no place to stay.

The *Hogares de Tránsito*

In 1948 Eva launched three temporary shelters (*hogares de tránsito*) in Buenos Aires. She was prompted by stories of migrant families living under bridges in the capital. The hogares opened after a first, preliminary shelter with housing for more than two hundred men, women, and children, within the Women's Hospital for the Insane, proved to be a disaster. In this first attempt the Sisters of the Garden (Hermanas del Huerto) aided Eva. All became horrified when women fought over the men and even traded husbands. Henceforth, only minor boys would live in the future hogares de tránsito, and men, other than the president and important guests, were only allowed to visit on holidays and for baptisms, communions, and weddings. Placed in upper-class neighborhoods, the hogares were lavishly furnished with everything from modest chamber pots to chandeliers as well as gifts that Juan and Eva received from foreign dignitaries. The furnishings purchased for the hogares came from the most elegant department stores, Gath y Chaves and Harrods, places where migrant women would never have shopped.[19]

After the new hogares de tránsito were established, thousands of women and children spent several days at a time in these lavish hostels, where Eva often appeared to greet them. Then she personally helped them find lodging, jobs, and schools for the children. The first one opened on April 3, 1948, and the second on June 19 of the same year, while the third home began accepting migrant women and children on August 14.[20] Juan Perón and his entire cabinet attended all three inaugural events, thereby directly linking the homes to the Peronist vision. Those sheltered in these centers often found immediate solutions for their problems, chapels in which to pray, catechism classes, and the hope of acquiring jobs, clothing, and household furnishings.

The documents show that Eva personally directed women who met her at the Foundation to the hogares de tránsito, and certain individuals came under her protection. Others simply mentioned that they had lodged at one of the homes. Edelina Orso de Balán, a thirty-five-year-old woman with four children and a bigamous husband, must have been one of the women who first lived under a bridge to move to housing in the early shelter set up at the hospital, as she resided there with her four children in June 1947. Originally from Córdoba province, she subsequently worked in Buenos Aires as a domestic servant earning a miserable 50 pesos per month after a portion of her debt to her employer was deducted. Under these circumstances Edelina felt she had little option other than placing her children into custodial care; that same month, one of her sons entered the General Martín Rodríguez home. According to the social worker's report, Edelina initially asked that all three sons be placed in boarding schools while she cared for her youngest, a daughter. Her relatives in Córdoba could not assume responsibility for the children, and their maternal grandmother, with whom they lived before, had died. These three sons remained in various institutions, where their mother visited them, until 1954.[21]

In 1949 a woman pleaded that the state allow her child to enter an orphanage. Analía Cuenta de Rivera, a widow, lived in one of the hogares de tránsito with her three sons. She had migrated from the interior and needed to send her children into care. Adela Candiani de Jensen, a social worker, had written the note that Analía carried with her. Two months later one of her sons entered the Hogar General José de San Martín, where he remained until October 1951.[22]

When it became clear that Jewish women were among the families in the hogares de tránsito, a Jewish women's philanthropic organization established its own hogar de tránsito for Jewish families migrating from the agricultural colonies of the interior to Buenos Aires. The adult women stayed in a wing of the Jewish Girls' Orphanage, where they benefited from classes in Hebrew and religion. This effort began with a 1,000-peso donation from a vice president of the Society of Beneficence of Jewish Ladies (Sociedad de Damas Israelitas de Beneficencia). The women who lodged at the Jewish hogar de tránsito received courses in religious instruction as well as business-related courses until they could support themselves. In the meantime, the Damas Israelitas helped them by providing sewing machines, lodging for the children, and medical care if needed. Fear of Catholic instruction had a definite impact on non-Catholic communities, pushing them away from Eva's hogares, and added to their anxieties about the return of religious education in the public schools instituted by General Pedro Ramírez in 1943 and supported by Juan.[23]

Eva also helped women who never made it to the hogares de tránsito. Julia Noriega de Kaufman's two children were sent to the Instituto Mercedes de Lasala y Riglos on December 5, 1947, at Eva's request to the Society of Beneficence to find appropriate institutions for Julia's minor children. Julia's older children also lived in institutions. The mother, at that time interned in a clinic, could not possibly care for the children, and her boyfriend, who had frequently been accused of violent assaults, had committed suicide. Both of the older boys went to the Hogar General Martín in June 1948. In this case, as in others, the children received aid as their mother entered a temporary shelter. Despite her illness, Julia wrote to her children to tell them about each other's progress, or lack thereof.[24]

In August 1948 the Eva Perón Foundation passed on information that Rita Martes, an impoverished woman who lived with her son in a wooden shed behind the fashionable furniture store that employed her in Buenos Aires, needed to inter her son in an orphanage as she could not take care of him. The father had abandoned them both, and she suffered from bronchitis—a common malady in Argentina, especially in Buenos Aires, during the winter months. The following month the son went to an orphanage, and in December Rita wrote him that Eva had not only given him a bicycle but also a house in which both of them could live.

> As a mother today I tenderly pray to God and I bless you every day. I hope you are well and are healthy; you don't know how anxious I am to see you and have a chance to have you at my side for a while so that I can kiss you and give you my advice. I hope you are behaving well and are good to your teachers and that you study. . . . Look for me on the first Sunday of January 1949. I am happy to tell you that I already have the little house that Sra. Evita Duarte de Perón gave to us. Thanks to her and to General Perón, I am already tranquil, and I am taking care of your bicycle. I send your little brother's kisses, and many hugs and kisses from your mother who never forgets you. God bless you in the coming year.[25]

The grandfather of a child abandoned by his parents wrote to Eva Perón pleading with her to place the child in an orphanage:

I am the guardian of a boy abandoned by his parents and I would like
to place him in a welfare school as I have noted in the Directorate of
Minors . . . but such a long time has passed without any word. My desire
is to educate him and have him in a boarding school because I am a
widower and have no woman to care for him, and my savings are scarce.
Furthermore, I am elderly and the salary for my job is a pittance.[26]

A social worker's report noted that Juan Victorio, the children's grandfather,
was sixty-eight and lived in a badly constructed room with his single daughter. He eked out an existence working part time for a barber. Consequently
the child went into the Manuel Roca Home in April 1950 and stayed there
until 1953.

Throughout the early years, letters to Eva typically involved women who
were mothers or who wanted to be. For example, in September 1947 Adriana
de Castro sought to adopt a child, a baby abandoned by its mother. In June
1948 she wrote to her "Excelentísima Sra. Doña Eva Duarte de Perón" that
after seven years of marriage, she had given up hope of becoming pregnant,
and for that reason wanted to "have a little girl under our custody." She used
this term because no laws existed to legitimate legal adoption. Until such a
law was passed, guardians who wished to transmit inheritance to their wards
had to falsify a child's birth certificate at the Civil Registry. Adriana wanted
to obtain her child legally, and the baby went to live with her. Only after a
Peronist-supported adoption law passed congress, in September 1948, could
would-be parents request complete legal adoption.[27]

Adoption was not the only problem confronted by the Peronist government. The desire of poor people to enroll their children in boarding schools
rather than public schools, as noted earlier, led to many parental petitions to
the Society of Beneficence. For example, in October 1947 Dr. Armando
Méndez San Martín received a letter from the National Bureau of Minors
(Dirección Nacional de Menores) with copies from to the Instituto Ángel T.
de Alvear, the Hogar de Niñas "Crescencia Boado de Garrigós," and the
Hogar General Martín Rodríguez.[28] The correspondence stated that Sra. Elenora de Mangioni had spoken with Eva, who had promised her that four of
her nine children, ages fifteen, fourteen, eleven, and nine, could be boarded
at a school in order to complete their elementary instruction and learn a
trade. Evidently Eva had agreed with the mother, telling her that Lt. Col.
Castro would find them appropriate places. However, according to Elenora,

Castro had put her children in schools that didn't prepare them properly. In another letter, she declared that her children still could not read. Elenora blamed the situation on the schools, not on her children, and thus felt "it appropriate before bothering Sra. (Perón) again, that I would let you know this."[29] Two years later the parents requested, and received, permission to withdraw the children from the boarding schools. This case showed that parents could have unreasonable expectations that the level of education received by children in institutional care exceeded that of public schools. Most parents, however, remained undeterred by this possibility.

In August 1948 José Carena wrote to Eva from Temperley, province of Buenos Aires, addressing her as "the First Lady of Social Works." José had one son, five years old, and no wife. He had gone to all the orphanages seeking a place for his son, so he finally decided to turn to Eva, "because you will know how complicated it is for a man to go to work with such a young son. Also I will tell you that I am experiencing several critical days because I cannot abandon him." José's file indicated that after the mother had abandoned the children, an aunt had cared for them for two years. Finally José's mother took control of her son's plight. She moved to Buenos Aires, sent for the son (who entered the Instituto Mercedes de Lasala y Riglos), and then moved to another home. We know that Eva had a part in placing the boy in a charitable boarding school, as the letter arrived with a memorandum from the presidential residence.[30] The publicity surrounding Eva's beneficence had spread beyond the national capital.

In 1949 the mother of twin sons sought to place them in appropriate institutions, and Eva's signature on the documents is testimony to her assistance in this case. The mother already had two other twin boys who were given beds, mattresses, and blankets by Eva. In addition, one of the ten-year-old twins who did not attend school behaved badly and was admitted to the Hogar General Martín Rodríguez where his mother and twin brother visited him from time to time. The home, located in the town of Berisso in the province of Buenos Aires, had opened in 1937 under the auspices of the National Child Protection Association (Patronato Nacional de Menores) developed by President Agustín P. Justo. By 1957 the boy resided in another institution and from there went to live with a foster family.[31]

Immigrant women also received help from Eva. María Cuenta, a Chilean, wrote to her in May 1951. María had traveled from Comodoro Rivadavia in the Patagonian south with her three young children. Her common-law husband, an Italian with a legal wife in Europe, had lived with María for fourteen years but was a womanizer who often drank too much and showed little affection for the children. Finally a pregnant María left him and made her way to Buenos Aires. Her letter to Eva indicated that the family was living in a hotel. Eva arranged for the eldest daughter to enter an orphanage, where she stayed until 1959. There her mother visited her regularly but never made enough money to keep her at home.[32]

Even victims of the 1944 San Juan earthquake still needed help. In one letter, addressed to Eva, a victim of the earthquake in 1949 wrote:

> After your visit to our Provinces, I believe that you . . . have been preoccupied with our great tragedy, one that still affects many families of San Juan despite the concerns of our Governor Godoy. He is a dynamic man who has not wasted an instant because of his preoccupation with . . . family housing and the authorization of lottery prizes. But we still remain without a home and without this solution today we hope for your generous hand to be extended to those in need and who are humble servants. . . .
>
> Our dear Evita it gives me great pleasure to write you because you have a good heart and you can help me. This letter is to ask that you resolve my problem because I cannot live here with my mother, my brothers, and my husband. We ask for a home as we must go and we have nowhere to go. I filled out paperwork to ask for a house in the Rivadavia neighborhood and they told me that for the moment that is not possible because they are very busy with other cases and they offered me a hut made out of cardboard so that I can put it somewhere, but I have no land to put it on and besides, there are many in our family and we have several young children. When you came to San Juan, I wanted to talk to you and I was not allowed to. I would like to live in a neighborhood that bears your name and despite our poverty we know how to behave ourselves in such a dignified neighborhood.[33]

Eva was so much more approachable than Juan or the municipal authorities of San Juan, who responded to traditional elites more rapidly than to the poor.[34]

Did Eva Replace or Take Over Other Charities?

All Eva's efforts to help workers and the poor did not mean that everyone had a safety net, and the First Lady's charitable empire, despite the avid demands of her supporters, never replaced other philanthropies. The poorest and most bereft fell between the cracks of bureaucracy.

The government-subsidized philanthropic system created in the nineteenth century thus overlapped the emerging Peronist welfare state, frequently creating confusion. Some examples from the 1940s demonstrate how people struggled to learn the difference between communicating with philanthropies and writing to Juan and Eva. In April 1945 the mother of Sara Jessica Partera (a pseudonym) went to the Society of Beneficence to ask that her daughter be interned in a school. The mother had migrated from Mendoza with all her children, and she blamed their problems on the "*mala vida*" (inappropriate lifestyle) of their father. At first the mother went to the brother of a friend, but he could not afford to support her five children. The damas of the Society of Beneficence sent Sara, then about two years old, to an external wet nurse.

According to the society's social worker, the mother lived "In a miserable house made of wood and zinc strips. She works as a seamstress, but earns little for her shirt repairs. The husband abandoned her and took clothing, furniture, and all the household goods, leaving her on the street with five children."[35] The social worker thought it was a crime that the family paid rent on such a wretched *pocilga* (pigsty), and if it had not been for the kindness of one of the daughter's employers, they probably would have starved.

This file underscores the principal issues confronting newly arrived migrant women and their families in the capital city. They had spouses or partners who had abandoned them. They supported minor children, and their relatives back at home usually found themselves in circumstances that were as difficult as Sara's deplorable situation. Finally, when women found housing in the capital city, it usually consisted of substandard and unhygienic conditions. For these reasons, the Society of Beneficence took in the youngest, including Sara and her twin sister. This story, worthy of the melodrama we find in tango lyrics, reveals individual problems rather than those of a group or class. Sara's story typified the personal stories that Eva eventually received.

After Perón became president and in the midst of his government's efforts to expropriate the Society of Beneficence, social workers employed there told the tale of municipal efforts to dislodge all 170 inhabitants from an overcrowded tenement house comprised of thirty-four rooms, that is, one room for every five tenants. In a letter related to this situation, the Ladies of Saint Vincent de Paul Society (Sociedad de Damas de San Vicente de Paul) wrote to the Society of Beneficence, seeking help for a family consisting of a mother, a paternal grandmother, and five children. They lived in one room with two beds. The social worker described the situation of one of the sons named Oscar:

> The future of the child is uncertain; his mother lacks the resources, the time, and the capacity to orient him. The child has no other prospects than to live in the street and play ball, but as he is clever and somewhat intelligent, I believe, and taking into account his young age, that if he lived in an appropriate place it would be easy to direct him, control his behavior, and discipline his activities. . . . During the day he stays alone with his brothers, lives on the street, and misbehaves like boys his age. Their mother leaves early for work and returns at seven p.m.[36]

The Society of Beneficence took Oscar to help the family, and the boy remained in a boarding school until January 1950.

From the province of Buenos Aires, Sra. Cecilia Bagneas, president of the Ladies of St. Vincent de Paul, wrote to the president of the Society of Beneficence in 1947, ignoring the fact that the Peronist Armando Méndez San Martín controlled the society. She asked that a local rural child, Carlos Pattinato, be awarded "of course if it is possible" a fellowship to attend the Instituto Ángel Torcuato de Alvear, a dependency of the Society of Beneficence in Luján. Twelve-year-old Carlos, according to Cecilia, was the son of "a terribly poor father" and his mother was "an exemplary woman who with Christian resignation abandoned her home to perform domestic service."[37] This language typified the moral tones that charities usually invoked to separate good families from "unacceptable" ones. The boy came from a family of five children and a handicapped father. Méndez San Martín evidently disregarded the fact that he was neither mentioned nor addressed in the petition; in February 1948, the boy went to study at the school in Luján, where he remained until 1953. Eventually other siblings were sent to boarding schools. This letter shows how religious groups helped families during the postwar depression and how the Society of Beneficence continued to function until 1948 even after it was taken over by the Peronists and became part of the welfare state.

A Greek baby, abandoned by his mentally challenged mother ("de origen griego, quien se suponía tenía las facultades mentales alteradas") entered the Society of Beneficence's foundling home in December 1947. The following year, the society made inquiries about the mother and found that she did not visit the child. She was well enough to work in a factory, but her pay was insufficient to enable her to make the trip to visit him. In time, with the justification that his mother's mental illness rendered her incapable of caring for him, the society allowed the child to live with foster parents who eventually adopted him.[38]

In 1948, in the midst of Peronist-proclaimed prosperity, Graciela García found herself in desperate straits and decided her only hope lay in moving from Gran Chaco territory to Buenos Aires. There, without the intercession of Eva or Juan, the Society of Beneficence took in Graciela and her two boys and a girl. The last notation in this case reveals that the family retrieved Graciela's son in 1952 and persuaded a judge to allow him to use his mother's surname.[39]

In 1950 a dying mother wrote to Eva from her hospital bed. A widow from the province of Buenos Aires, Florencia desperately wanted to die in peace with the knowledge that her two minor boys, aged ten and eleven, would not become abandoned and unwanted. She hoped that with Eva's help, the two would become "good men and proud of their country." Because she was illiterate, the local police affirmed that the letter was signed with her fingerprint. Investigations by social workers found the boys abandoned and determined that they had been born in Córdoba. Their mother died shortly thereafter. Their paternal aunt visited the orphaned children. Thus, the mother received her dying wish.[40]

My extensive examination of over one thousand children's files from the Society of Beneficence and other state agencies, dated from 1880 to 1955, revealed absolutely no discrimination against those who did not have the support of Juan and Eva. What these letters do show is how families became deeply affected by national and international economic conditions and how mothers often became the principal support for their families. When they could no longer cope, they often sought succor from others. This led many to write to the First Lady. They addressed her in many ways, displaying degrees of closeness or distance in terms of station in life. Most did not use the familiar "Evita," and none reveal an assumption that Eva controlled the Society of Beneficence.

Eva's Presumed Nemesis, the Society of Beneficence

A major tactic that led to new relationships between the Peróns and the people came about through Juan's intervention in the Society of Beneficence.[41]

This was a slow and conflictive process, since rumors circulated of the elite women's animosity toward Eva, and Eva showed clear signs she wanted to change the hierarchical nature of charity. But she did not have the authority to close the society down. At the same time, Juan did not want to openly challenge the women's group, preferring a smooth transition to a welfare state, but he was the only one who could put an end to the society's control. From 1946 to 1948 the Society of Beneficence remained in limbo while Juan and Eva's supporters, on the other hand, became increasingly restive and eager to do away with the society. The tensions between Juan and Eva, as well as spoken and written critiques of the society, interfered with the establishment of charismatic politics.

Thus, in the early years, President Perón began to intrude in areas formerly controlled by the Society of Beneficence. On November 27, 1943, the military government instituted Decree 14.074/43, creating the National Department of Social Assistance (Departamento Nacional de Previsión Social), which folded in the Department of Labor and Department of Social Assistance as well as several other entities and placed Perón in charge. This maneuver created problems for the Society of Beneficence, as it originally was housed under the Ministry of Foreign Relations and Religion, where it received political protection. Henceforth part of the society came under the jurisdiction of the Ministry of the Interior, while its hospitals fell under the control of the National Department of Social Assistance.

Subsequently, new worries confronted the society. In June 1946 rumors began to circulate revealing that former inmates of the society's institutions who had hoped to become its employees were furious over personnel changes. After many years of hiring former clients on that basis alone, the women who directed the society began to hire on the basis of competence. With few jobs around for people who rarely attended school beyond the primary years, ex-clients wanted their sinecures.

Indeed, on September 6 Juan named Méndez San Martín to oversee and reorganize the Society of Beneficence rather than close it down. Méndez San Martín had joined the Peronist cause after militating in the conservative provincial administration of Manuel Fresco, a public health physician who combined right-wing ideology with notions of an extensive welfare state.[42] For Méndez San Martín, expansion and state control of the Society of Beneficence seemed logical.

As shown in a 1946 document, government control over the society was supposed to become the keystone of a new, rationalized welfare state. The Integral Plan (Plan Integral) proposed by Méndez San Martín (who held the government position of intervener) put the society at the top of a pyramid. The institution would be transformed by merging national and Buenos Aires social assistance into its structure. Then the society and all beneficent societies would be linked to government subsidies and to the National Lottery. This reform plan, on a more modest level, had been suggested in the 1930s and then rejected by the society, so members of the Sociedad de Damas de San Vicente de Paul at first felt confident that they could outflank reform plans.

What neither Méndez San Martín, nor Perón, nor the damas had counted upon was the pent-up anger toward the society on the part of Peronist legislators and the Peronist press. Filled with class anger over the use of public funds so that elite women could perform charity, they simply could not accept the possibility that the group would remain a viable entity under Peronism and that the women would not be punished by Peronist populism.

The only way Perón could prevent an open confrontation among himself, the damas, and his supporters was to avoid meeting with the women. Such meetings would either have been interpreted as the president caving in to the damas or as a continuation of the presidential tradition that always granted

CHART 4. Comprehensive Plan (Plan Integral)

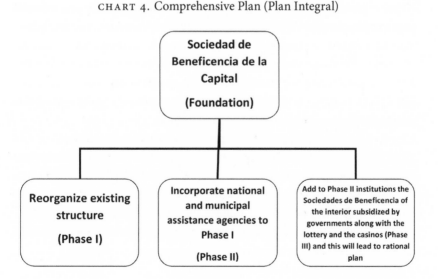

the petitions of the society. The damas did not have an audience with the president until September 18, 1946, when forty of them went to the Casa Rosada to meet with him. At that time, according to a report in *La Prensa* found in the official file on the intervention, President Perón "expressed that the Society of Beneficence was necessary for the country" and promised not to remove from their offices the physicians who worked for the entity.[43] At that time, according to the report of the president of the society, Perón tried to calm the fears of the damas by claiming that:

> Government efforts were not intended to weaken the Society of Beneficence. Rather they were intended to restructure the group under the supervision of the Intervener in order to expand the Institution at the same time that it added a more democratic leadership. The new statutes mandated that the Society coordinate its activities with government services. However the basic elements of the organization, according to the president, would remain so that the group could continue its social function with the same sense of responsibility that had always guided it. . . . The president also added that the Society was part of an Argentine tradition that should be maintained.[44]

Had Perón lied to the women? Had he really intended to keep the society intact and allow the women to participate in the activities of its institutions? According to the organizational diagram, he had not lied, but his actions shortly after intervening in the society argue otherwise. Furthermore, the Peronist governor of the province of Buenos Aires, Domingo Mercante, and his newspaper *El Laborista* had other plans. Long before Eva Perón became the champion of the poor and disenfranchised, Mercante, who was particularly sensitive to social welfare issues, expressed a clear vision of an ideal welfare-state society and used his position both as governor and as editor to promote his ideas. *El Laborista* envisioned working-class women who raised their children to be patriotic citizens and Argentina as a country where these women and their families would have the right to affordable housing.[45] The paper published a variety of editorials and articles supportive of a caring welfare state. In May 1946 the newspaper defended the creation of the Secretariat of Public Health as well as efforts by legislators to promote a child adoption law in Argentina.[46]

Through his newspaper, Mercante fueled working-class anger against the society. On July 11, 1948, *El Laborista* claimed that many former inmates of the society's institutions had bitter memories of their experiences and accused the society of having little tenderness for them.[47] On August 3, the newspaper continued its critique with a picture of an indigent woman sitting in the street with a baby in her arms and a barefoot boy of about four years of age by her side. Peronists accused the society of ignoring such women and children.[48] Even more revealing, they claimed that the campaign against the society should be attributed to *El Laborista*'s publishers, not to Eva Perón. As they put it, "La Sra. María Eva Duarte de Perón, whose support we have solicited, has recognized our claims in this anxious clamor, assuring us that she will exert all her influence in this matter as soon as possible."[49] Either this was an effort to minimize Eva's role or it reflected Mercante's sincere belief that, among Peronists, he was the most committed to closing down the society. In fact, when the decree abolishing the society passed, the newspaper directly took credit for it with headlines that proclaimed a victory for the journal and mentioned that Eva Perón was ill and unable to be seen in public.

Intervener Méndez San Martín continued to meet with the damas, and his original plan included an expanded board that included the damas plus female representatives from labor unions and other groups. The new board would then elect its own president.[50] While this plan seemed satisfactory to Méndez San Martín and might have even been approved by Juan Perón, others, like Mercante, wanted to punish the society and end its activities once and for all. As an unfavorable report on Méndez San Martín's document explained, "The main problem with the [Méndez de San Martín] proposal is the fact that the governance of the Society would practically be handed over to the damas who have been running it since it was intervened."[51] Clearly multiple and antagonistic opinions circulated among Peronists regarding the society and whether the damas of the society, as well as the philanthropic entity, would be useful or a hindrance to Peronism. Eva had nothing to do with this battle.

Did Perón want to create a totally new form of pension? The answer seems to be yes, since President Perón on September 6, 1946, intervened in the society. He then expanded and refined the new category of subsidies to the poor in November 1946, although it took a while for people to notice the change. In the meantime, Juan asked that the society women prepare reports on the situation in their various institutions. On December 7, 1946, they delivered the reports and inquired about the specific role that the newly named Women's Advisory Commission (Junta de Damas) would play. The society's minutes reported that the intervener and other government delegates

> intended to keep the Society in charge of the direction, administration, and supervision of all the dependencies of the institution, with broad powers to inspect according to current statutes. The statements were absolutely clear, leaving the impression that the Advisory Commissions will evaluate the work accomplished by the Society.[52]

Perón then invited the women to organize a special exposition to show the contribution the group had made to Argentina. He offered the venue of the government petroleum-monopoly building. The women took him seriously and opened the exposition in the lobby of the building on December 23, with the president and other dignitaries in attendance. All this took place after Perón had announced his revolutionary plans to transform Argentina. Yet the damas continued to meet with Méndez San Martín until April 30, 1947. Evidently the women represented a far thornier issue than anyone had imagined.

With Decree 15.590/46, issued on November 6, 1946, Perón established that anyone who wanted a pension or a subsidy had to present themselves with appropriate documents to the Institute for Social Welfare. This meant that the system of congressional petitions would end, although it did not specifically deny the Society of Beneficence the right to give out old-age assistance. The society's matrons responded by changing their pension's name. Henceforth, the secretary of the society suggested that *decenas* (lottery tenths, perhaps to reflect the notion of tithing to religious charity, or *diezmos*) should henceforth be called beneficent subsidies (*subsidios de beneficencia*), a decision that the president supported and incorporated into the group's statutes.[53] The president kept the society women working to save their own group while he faced his opponents and then decreed the formation of new welfare benefits.

The early years of Peronism might have appeared to outsiders, as well as to opponents inside Argentina, as the beginnings of a fascist government under a popularly elected president. The rise in popularity of his wife, Eva, signaled to anti-Peronists that an upstart illegitimate movie star would become the hope for the disenfranchised and poor, as well as a target of the unforgiving middle and upper classes. Juan and Eva also had to deal with the pent-up populism of the rural poor as seen in the early years of correspondence between lower-class folk sketched in this chapter. The question ultimately became one of balance—between the aspirations of people to reach to the Peróns personally and the desire of the Peróns to respond in an appropriate fashion. The letter writing encouraged earlier by Yrigoyen became transformed into a political mechanism to maintain charismatic links between Argentines and their leaders.

After Perón came to power the Society of Beneficence remained faithful to many of its supplicants until it finally lost control of its institutions in 1948. Society homes and hospitals were folded into the government bureaucracy. Eva never controlled the society's institutions, despite the clamors from Eva's devoted followers to turn everything over to her. In early 1948 Eva Perón's name was invoked in a petition to Méndez San Martín by the niece of two women who had been receiving charitable monies from the society since 1910, but Eva had nothing to do with the disposition of the request. The two women petitioners, orphaned at an early age, had received subsidies from the Society of Beneficence. The correspondence submitted provided a long chain of antecedents for the daughter of one of the women to ask that the subsidy received by the aunt who raised her be transferred to the niece. Evidently the niece had cared for her mother and aunt, and the combined subsidies had helped pay the rent while the elderly ladies had lived off of their abilities to sew. The niece received her subsidy.[54] Juan Perón might have closed down the institution, but his government remained sensitive to its clients. One of Eva's last interactions took place in May 1952 when she met a young man, Abel, who identified himself as a missionary, evidently of Peronism, without further elaboration. At that time, Eva helped the man secure a job as a mechanic in the city of Posadas, Misiones, with the Argentine Airlines. After she died, he wrote to the head of the Ministry of Technical Affairs, Raúl Mende, asking for another favor. In the December letter he referred to Eva as "his second mother for having fought for my future as a mechanic." He believed that the humble still received messages from her, just as he had sent a cargo of bananas to Eva. Now he wanted to ask Juan for money to purchase a plot of land so that he could marry and start a family. If not, he wanted to meet with the president personally. Documents indicate that he was told to file a formal request for a loan with the National Land Bank (Banco Hipotecario Nacional).

Evidently Abel never got to meet Juan, although he kept writing. By May 1953 Abel received orders from Argentine Airlines to move to Buenos Aires, which he did not want to do. Thus he wrote several more times to Minister Mende. On several letters he created his own stationery to show his allegiance to the Peróns.

In July he sent yet another letter requesting the intercession of Juan to help him stay in Posadas. The Argentine airline company made Abel's wish come true by allowing him to remain in Posadas, but it is unclear if he ever received a loan.[55]

Abel's case demonstrates several important points. First of all, the early correspondence between Abel and Eva has disappeared, an indication that many letters indeed disappeared in the aftermath of Juan's overthrow in 1955. Secondly, it shows how people voluntarily sought out Eva's aid, in contrast to the letters that Juan solicited. It is evident that the letters beseeched the First Lady to resolve emotionally loaded issues related to family survival. The "bridge of love" described by Maryssa Navarro was not constructed by Eva, but rather by the people. More letters to Eva appear subsequently throughout the book, and they verify how important Eva's charismatic bridge became, even when it was a sham, as seen in the next chapter.

Thus Peronism learned to combine the old with the new ways of promoting communication, and Juan, Eva, and their supporters had to adjust. While Juan would have preferred a relatively impersonal bureaucratic response to individual needs, Eva's performance of charity helped fill an important need that Juan himself came to recognize. Perhaps this was the battle between a modernized charismatic state and and an impersonal welfare state. Charisma could not be eliminated from the Argentine political equation, but it could be refined. As we will see, Juan himself came to recognize this when he set up an old-age subsidy plan to replace earlier schemes of the Society of Beneficence, letting Eva's charitable foundation hand out the extremely modest sums.

Equally important, letters from these supplicants indicate that people had their own ideas about how government should operate. Rather than a bureaucracy, they wanted personal contact with their leaders. The very poor who migrated did not want to send their children to public schools as envisioned by Sarmiento. Instead, parents wanted children sent to boarding schools where they would benefit from housing, food, and medical care. They also used traditional metaphors such as the need to promote patriotism among children, seen in chapter 5, to appeal to their leaders. The very poor wanted to share their suffering, misery, and private dilemmas, but they did so on their terms. In some ways, these letters are similar to contemporary television programs wherein people tell the audience their toils and troubles. As a result, they are rewarded with the largess coming from program sponsors.

These letters to Eva, focusing mostly on the needs of children, showed a feminine side to early Peronism. Mothers pleaded with Eva and received all kinds of help from a woman who had no children of her own, and these letters reaffirm Omar Acha's views on sentimental and melodramatic maternalism during this time.[56] As will be seen in the next chapter, these unsolicited letters contrast greatly with others sent, despite a bureaucratic process, directly to Eva.

CHAPTER 2

Pensions for the Elderly and Infirm

NO MATTER HOW popular the new president appeared to be, political realities often meant that the legislative path to implementing his goals seemed daunting. Such was the case with the pensions for the elderly and infirm, a very popular early Peronist program that was rarely commented on. Newspapers in the capital city most likely did not pay attention to the pensions because of who became the principal recipients—rural unemployed and elderly poor people. The pension issue was sensitive, as the president was also trying to limit the influence of the great sacred cow of Argentine philanthropy, the Society of Beneficence. Thus, rather than deal with another contentious legislative skirmish, on November 6, 1946, President Perón invoked Decree No. 15.515 to rationalize the payment of subsidies to poor and infirm people and ensure that everyone was treated fairly.

Before then only select workers received old-age pensions through their own profession-related pension funds (e.g., railroad workers, power and light workers), while widows of military men and others needed to petition congress for these benefits. Poor people depended upon the charity of the Society of Beneficence or another of the more than three thousand immigrant and religious organizations that had evolved in the early twentieth century. However, the modernization of the state in the 1930s, accompanied by a decline in immigration at the same time that labor unions began to offer more social benefits than ever before, meant that immigrant mutual-aid societies and charities of all different types started to suffer from overexpansion at a time when their constituency shrank. Workers now paid union dues, and the number of both blue- and white-collar workers receiving pensions increased dramatically. Pregnant women received coverage after the legislative creation of a modest national Mothers' Pension Fund (Caja de Maternidad) in 1934. The fund also provided funds for working mothers during their maternity leave, mostly paid out of their own salaries. Increasingly, subsidies for old age and infirmities became one of the only ways that the unemployed, those who could not apply for union funds, and the elderly could receive benefits.[1]

For the very poor in the capital city, the municipality of Buenos Aires had developed a modern public-assistance program that began in the 1890s and provided medical care for the poor, women, and infants living there. The province of Buenos Aires, under the fascist governor Manuel Fresco (1936–1940), a physician, also created extensive welfare facilities that were extended during the Peronist administration by Col. Domingo Mercante (1946–1952).[2]

Other provinces, however, did not have adequate economic resources to offer welfare to their inhabitants, and this partly explained the increased migration to Buenos Aires during that time. In Buenos Aires, most of the needy by the 1940s were Argentine migrant women or elderly immigrants, many of whom had lost touch with their homelands after living for decades in Argentina. In the interior, however, elderly inhabitants, along with the sick and poor, had neither the means nor the ability to migrate. To make up for the limited access experienced by the poor outside Buenos Aires, provincial Societies of Beneficence had sprung up but had far less funding. While most Peronist legislation has been seen as a way to promote the well-being of the working class in Buenos Aires, Decree 15.515, Charitable Subsidies (Subsidios de Beneficencia), became a stopgap, irrational measure to reduce migration and provide a government safety net to the elderly, poor, and infirm. This meant that Perón could expand old-age pensions while battling the Society of Beneficence that prided itself on limiting its charitable activities to the capital city.

Like many of Perón's programs discussed in his five-year plan, the new subsidy law took a long time to implement because the government simply did not have the networks necessary to provide such services. This provided an opportunity for the Eva Perón Foundation to expand its influence in the interior. Eva and her foundation handed out the pensions publicly after 1950, even though the government paid for them through implementation of the decree. In this way, the weakness of the welfare state cemented Eva's charismatic bonds to people in the interior.

The subsidies came in three categories—A, B, and C, paying from 50 to 150 pesos per month, respectively—supposedly determined by age, the number of minor children or other dependents, and whether people suffered infirmities. Before the inflation of the 1950s, 150 pesos could support a family in the interior, but not in Buenos Aires. Thus, these pensions were meager at best and designed to help most infirm and elderly remain in lodgings they didn't own without the need to move to new localities where they had no family or community. Although many Argentines wrote to the national government seeking help in their old age, this subsidy was more than an old-age pension, because young mothers could apply. Eventually men and women of all ages applied for what the documents in the archives call both subsidies and pensions. The numbering of the case files is extremely inconsistent and many have several numbers. Since no lists identify who had subsidies and for how long, it is impossible to ascertain how many applied, how many were turned down, or how long the subsidies lasted. Nevertheless, the implementation of a national subsidy presaged the replacement of the Societies of Beneficence and charities as the main source of aid for people with all kinds of problems.

Before receiving a pension, as a minimum requisite candidates needed to submit a certification of poverty, a medical certificate if they were under sixty, a sworn declaration, and proof of property rental. If they were homeless, that, too, had to be verified. All pensions came from the Ministry of Labor and Social Welfare, Department of Social Assistance (whose name later changed), and all petitioners were supposed to present their documents at that ministry. The decree was a masterpiece of bureaucratic formulations to replace pious charities where people had to prove not only how poor they were, but also how much they had suffered.

As most of the people who applied for these funds lived outside Buenos Aires and comprised the poorest and least-educated inhabitants, it took a while for people to learn the new system. As a vestige of the Society of Beneficence, Article 7 mandated that pensions not be given to people who did not live "an honest life," although no evidence exists that this article provided a moral litmus test, and even people who had lived in unmarried relationships qualified. Instead, those who owned real estate or received pensions of 50 or more pesos were excluded, but enforcement of this provision was haphazard.[3] Unless petitioners met these requirements, the subsidies were supposed to be off limits—that is, until charismatic politics began to cloud the situation because of the unclear relationship between the Department of Social Assistance and the Eva Perón Foundation.

Although the decree defined these payments as subsidies, most of the people who applied for them called them pensions. Equally important, early requests were submitted not on forms but through letters to Juan and, especially, to Eva, despite the impersonal and bureaucratic language of the decree. Furthermore, after its creation, many petitioners wrote to the Eva Perón Foundation and asked its local representatives to intercede for them in pension cases. The Social Assistance Department frequently allowed the Eva Perón Foundation to send out notices of subsidies and permitted Eva to dole these out to qualified people who had not completed application forms, with the expectation that the recipients would still comply with the law. And yet many files indicate that the Eva Perón Foundation refused to handle such requests, advising petitioners to go to the Social Assistance Department. At this juncture, the Society of Beneficence had no part in the assessment of cases or distribution of pensions, even though it still functioned until 1948.

People with Argentine minor children, as well as those who had served the country but had not received pensions, would have priority access to these funds; among these, widows took precedence. Confusion regarding these pensions or subsidies abounded, compounded by the government's closing of several important newspapers. Thus the media could not announce the bureaucratic requirements or even comment on the executive order. Applicants had to prove their inability to work, their economic need, and their general living, family, and health conditions. The government authorized the pensions, but few knew about them until Eva announced the first grantees in 1950.[4]

Widows seemed to have the ear of both Eva and the government bureaucracy. After all, Peronist views on women mandated that their biological mission superseded everything else. In *El Laborista*, Domingo Mercante particularly deplored the plight of abandoned children and asserted that families, rather than institutions, should care for them. Thus he vigorously led the campaign to close down the Society of Beneficence. And as far as working women were concerned, everything should be subordinated to motherhood.

In January 1946 the newspaper commented that despite the need to free women from the condition in which they had found themselves for centuries, women's liberation and education were necessary "because we understand that only in this way can women be efficient in the home and as mothers. Only this way can they be a dignified companion to men, and only this way can they useful to their patria."[5] If women served their nation well as wives, then it was also a patriotic duty of the state to care for them and their children after they lost their male breadwinners. This situation was particularly acute for the poor who seldom had property or savings and whose partners had abandoned them. Women who had not participated in the economy full time often found themselves in precarious positions later on in life.

Financial sleight of hand made the funding origin of these pensions very murky. For example, in December 1947, a surplus remained in the lottery fund of the Society of Beneficence allocated for poor pensions. Dr. Méndez San Martín ingratiated himself with Eva Perón by offering her organization María Eva Duarte de Perón Social Aid (Ayuda Social María Eva Duarte de Perón) the remaining 8,000 pesos. Eva graciously accepted the money, and we have one of the few documents with her signature attesting to the receipt of the donation.[6]

This transaction most likely reinforced Eva's desire to promote direct communication between herself and petitioners for assistance. It certainly shows how she and her admirers could circumvent legal boundaries. Furthermore, it appears that the new pensions did not begin to be granted in a public fashion until March 1950, when Eva publicly announced that one thousand people would become recipients of the new old-age pensions. Many impoverished individuals might have applied for years before they actually received a payment, although some cases received immediate attention. No logic governed how quickly the government responded to applications.

All people who applied, regardless of nationality, age, or degree of infirmity, were expected to fill out an extensive questionnaire. The form asked for information on citizenship, relatives, children, and place of residence. If applicants received help from relatives or neighbors, they had to list the amounts received. Sections of the form had to be filled out by social workers, members of the Eva Perón Foundation, or local authorities regarding the degree of medical need and quality of housing available for the applicant. The forms provide an unusual survey of poverty in 1940s and 1950s rural Argentina. Remarkably, these archives bring to life the stories of countless people who had not benefited from urban education and the rise of a modern economy.

A clear example of how the rules could be flouted comes from a petition unaccompanied by a letter. Within the questionnaire the petitioner, a widow with children, admitted that she owned a rancho, though she was behind in her payments. She evidently went to see Eva at the Casa Rosada, where Eva promised to arrange for the payments. Eva also sent her a mattress, clothing, money, and food, along with 150 pesos. In addition, Eva promised the thirty-five-year-old widow that she could obtain a 100-peso pension to help her and her three minor children. On January 31, 1951, she was granted that pension despite the fact that she owned her own home, evidence that people fared far better if they could obtain a personal interview with Eva. However, establishing a charismatic link with her was a feat only a few of the many petitioners could achieve.[7]

Subsidies as Old-Age Pensions

The documents offer several early stories of the elderly. In the 1940s the term "elderly" had many meanings. Some defined the adjective as a person over the age of sixty, while others made distinctions between older people who could work and those who no longer could support themselves or their families. The decree itself demanded medical proof of need only for people under sixty. Nevertheless, many individuals in their fifties and even in their thirties applied for what they considered to be old-age pensions, usually because of health problems exacerbated by the burden of supporting children who had been born without the benefit of legal marriage. This also indicated that the level of public health outside Buenos Aires differed greatly from that of the capital city, especially in relationship to illegitimacy.

Some petitioners wrote to Juan and Eva about problems with their official requests or rights to obtain pensions. On May 23, 1946, an elderly widow asked the president for help regarding not her own pension but one that had been taken away from her husband while he was alive:[8]

I am a sixty-five-year-old widow with two unmarried daughters. All three of us are sick; one is epileptic and has frequent attacks that make it impossible for her to work. The second suffers from a nervous condition, aggravated by her increasing deafness. We have no resources and survive performing domestic chores, but for the reasons mentioned before, we cannot work much. For these reasons we lead extremely frugal lives, and suffer from all kinds of privations. I have been married to Juan Antonio Asta since 1914, who worked for the Police of the Province of Buenos Aires and who died in September 1940. As a widow I should receive a pension. For this reason I began a legal suit but they won't grant me one.

She went on to cite the law that says the government can deny a pension to "anyone who has been fired with reason for not being able to fulfill the responsibilities of his office." The records regarding the pension included a 1940 police report, issued shortly before her husband died, indicating that someone denounced him for drunkenness. "They claimed that my husband had infringed the law at a hearing where he was not represented, and even though he was gravely ill, they made him sign a statement to that effect and he died thirteen days later."

I can assure Sr. Colonel that what happened was completely unjust. My husband performed his duties for twenty-five years, and during that time he paid into his pension plan. But we cannot claim his pension because of a false accusation they made against [him] in a way that can be easily understood to be an attack against the family. In some way or another our family also contributed our support for the payment of these pension payments. There are favorable reports in the pension case, such as the one in which the chief of police expressed that the defendant never appeared drunk at work and that he performed his duties correctly.

Sr. Colonel, I am desperate; I don't know what to do; we cannot continue living like this. The attorney who represented me suggested that we take this before the Supreme Court of the Province; but I have no funds to do this and he has told me there are no other legal recourses.

However, I know that you can help me. I have followed and fought for your victorious defeat of your rival. I have heard about your works and I have faith that if you want to help me with this issue, it can be arranged. It can't be possible that anyone can oppose the intentions of the Colonel and what he is trying to do for his people. The facts demonstrate this.

For all these reasons, and following an impulse from my heart and the confidence that you can solve this, I beg you to respect the present letter, hoping you will resolve this situation.

I take the opportunity to salute you Sr. Colonel and your dignified wife and I wish you the best of fortune. . . .

It is clear from this letter that María Melo de Asta, the elderly widow, thought it was more proper to direct her letter to Juan rather than Eva. However, we know from the bureaucratic response from the province of Buenos Aires that the provincial court had already decided the case. The only way this woman might get a pension would be if the president influenced the governor of the province to intervene in the matter, but no documents survive to indicate whether Perón took this course of action. Furthermore, no one seems to have informed Sra. de Asta that a new subsidy for the poor existed. Most likely this woman received no aid from Juan or Eva. Neither the personal support mechanisms nor institutional means contemplated, but not yet enacted, in the five-year plan yielded results for Sra. de Asta.

An abandoned woman from Santa Fe province had better luck, as she wrote her letter in 1949 at a time when the subsidy paperwork at the Eva Perón Foundation functioned smoothly. Petrona Ríos Monte penned a short letter to Eva, addressing her as "muy distinguida y caritativa madre argentina" (the very distinguished and benevolent Argentine mother) and pouring out her story of misery and woe. Abandoned by her husband many years earlier and left alone to support her elderly mother, Petrona concluded her letter, "La Saluda con todo mi respeto y cariño que dentro de mi ancianidad soy Peronista" (I greet you as an elderly Peronist with all my respect). The Eva Perón Foundation granted her an "A" subsidy on July 9, 1950, Independence Day in Argentina.[9]

Of course, not everyone managed to get Eva's attention, a reality that attested to her reliance on friends for help, a resource that was far too limited. On September 19, 1949, a woman wrote directly to Eva after she had already sent two letters to her foundation. By this time the simple salutations found in early letters had begun to change, thereby acknowledging the power that Eva was perceived to wield. In this letter, the petitioner, as in many others, addressed the wife of the president as Her Excellency, the Very Dignified Sra. María Eva Duarte de Perón. The utilization of superlatives enhanced her dignity and elevated her status, as did the use of the formal name Eva rather than "Evita"—the name used in correspondence most often by people representing themselves as workers. She clearly embodied distinctive meanings for different groups. Those who addressed Eva with inflated titles identified her with the power inherent in her position as the wife of the president and the leader of her own organization, while the use of "Evita" acknowledged her humble background and her connectedness to the working class.

This petition from Petronella Sánchez from Santa Rosa, La Pampa, reveals that she had begun to seek aid in 1948. While Sra. Sánchez acknowleged the distance between herself and Eva, she used the personal form, *vos*, rather than *usted*, to create a fictive bond of intimacy between them:

> Even though I have written twice to the Social Aid agency you head . . . I write again so that you can help another poor person who needs it. I am seventy years old, I live alone, and I'm helpless. In effect, Sra., I survive only by washing the few items of clothing that neighbors give me. But now I realize I am too old to work, and I suffer from rheumatism.
>
> I went to the local office of the Secretariat of Labor and Welfare in this city, but it's been a while and no one comes to tell me any good news. Thus I ask for a thousand pardons from you, the Dignified Lady, and I ask with all my heart that you take pity on a poor old lady, and enable me to live my last years in comfort.

Once again no response is recorded. This woman would not have been able to benefit from the situation that developed later, when the crossed signals between the Secretariat of Labor and Welfare and the Eva Perón Foundation enabled Eva to give out temporary old-age pensions while recipients filled out the necessary forms.[10] This stemmed from the fact that the foundation's office initially was housed in the Secretariat of Labor and Welfare. In addition to this physical proximity, many people wrote to both institutions for old-age pensions.

An elderly illiterate woman from Mendoza asked someone to write Eva of her plight. The typewritten script most likely came from a notary. As Valentina explained, she did not write for herself, but rather for her two children, Iván and Beatriz, neither of whom could support themselves, and neither could she. Her letter arrived with a certificate of poverty that specifically stated that it should be sent to the Eva Perón Foundation. In addition to the certificate, the obligatory form indicated that her son was thirty-five and suffered from an illness so debilitating that his mother still had to feed and dress him. Iván received a 50-peso pension, but no paperwork remains regarding his sister.[11]

Another elderly illiterate woman from Corrientes had a neighbor write a letter to Eva on July 31, 1951. She indicated that she had written to the First Lady before and had received a response telling her to write to the agency in charge of subsidies rather than to her. Thus Elena Lazare again petitioned for some help. Without mentioning her age, she said that she lived alone, had no relatives, and did not have the strength to work for her daily bread and clothing because she was ill. Elena provided her identity-card number, but only the letter telling her desperate story remains in the archive. Eva was ill at the time and likely couldn't handle the volume of requests she received.[12] These two cases demonstrate that illiteracy was not an impediment to communication with the leaders of Argentina, because even in rural areas many literate people were willing to help the less fortunate communicate.

Family members also assisted the elderly, but sometimes they could help no longer. Edgardo Martínez, a carpenter from Paraná, had spent his entire life taking care of his mother. Now that he had reached the age of sixty-two, he needed aid because he could find no work. He had already petitioned the governor of the territory. His eighty-two-year-old mother, suffering from rheumatism for the past four years, barely had the energy to take care of the house. The two of them lived on 100 pesos per month. Edgardo submitted his request in October 1950 but did not receive the subsidy until May 1951, when he was awarded a 50-peso "A" pension.[13]

That same month a fifty-two-year-old woman from the capital city who suffered from cardiac disease wrote to Eva addressing her as "La Primera Dama Argentina." She identified herself as an "argentina peronista soltera" (a Peronist single woman). Her paperwork indicated that her parents, no longer living, were Italian immigrants. She had worked as a "profesora de labores" (a teacher who corrected homework of some sort), a profession she could no longer practice because she had cataracts. Based upon her medical history, she received an old-age pension as well. Was she elderly? These pensions were extremely flexible and often arbitrary.[14]

One of the few cases I encountered that recorded a negative response was that of a sixty-two-year-old single woman from Mendoza province who had worked all her life. Seemingly destined to work forever, she wrote, "I have absolutely no resources that work might provide me and because my health is precarious and I feel worn out because I am no longer young, I am left with no resources to continue the struggle for life." Ana María lived with a niece where she labored without salary to keep the house clean. The social worker's report concluded, "She really has everything she wants and yet still feels the need to be independent." For this reason she should not be complaining.[15]

In 1948 a twenty-six-year-old woman wrote directly to the Society of Beneficence for a pension. She lived in the province of Buenos Aires with a disabled, much older Spanish immigrant who could no longer work at the age of fifty-three. They had one child together, and he had two children from a previous relationship who lived with them as well. Despite the fact the couple had never married, making the children illegitimate, and because of a positive report from the caseworker, in April 1948 the woman received a "B" subsidy of 100 pesos.[16]

Men and Women with Dependent Children

The transitional situation of the Society of Beneficence, amid government intervention, coincided with Eva's first hogar de tránsito. One of the inhabitants, a Spanish immigrant who resided in Buenos Aires province, had a wife and six children under the age of twelve. He had been hospitalized in Buenos Aires and had a tracheotomy that left him with a breathing hole in his throat. To support his children he worked as a newspaper vendor, but he did not earn enough. Consequently the Society of Beneficence (finally closed in 1948) recommended him for a pension, and he was awarded a "B" subsidy of 100 pesos per month by the government. Supposedly he received this in October 1948, making him one of the very first pension or subsidy recipients.[17]

On November 2, 1947, a woman from the Chaco sent a letter to President Perón in search of a poor pension. A single mother with three sons and three daughters ranging from five months to thirteen years old, she had reached an impasse:[18]

> Three of my children attend school but sometimes they can't because their clothing needs to be washed and some are so tattered or they have

no shoes to wear. At other times, they don't go to school because we have
no bits of bread or cheese to fool their hunger. I have been ill for ten years
and, according to the doctors, suffer from sinusitis and need to go to
Buenos Aires for an operation. How could this be possible, my President,
for a poor woman such as myself, who cannot take care of my daily
needs, to go off to such a hospital in such a city? For the past seven years
I have been with a man of property here in the locale of Makelli and I
help in harvesting and he allows me to live in a rancho without charging
me. I haven't even the money to plant a banana tree and we live in a low-
lying area where rains prevent me from planting anything. And this is all
because I have nowhere to go and my children, during the rainy season,
have to sleep without covers on the floor. Sr. President, I ask you to help
me with some money, or with a job.

No answer has been recorded for this letter, despite the fact that the president
was already working on a more systematic method to provide aid for the
poor. It appears that other than through the direct cash subsidies from Eva
or through the renamed diezmos handed out by the Society of Beneficence
(until it was finally closed down in 1948), the new pensions or subsidies often
remained unavailable or inconsistently administered.

Because of this long delay, as well as unexplained glitches in the system,
sometimes people had to write several times, and even this did not guarantee
help. In August 1948 a fourteen-year-old boy wrote to the minister of education complaining that Eva, whom he called Evita, had not answered his
request for a scholarship even though he was one of three orphans without
aid. "I can't earn a living . . . as you will see in my picture that I sent that I
have no right arm and it is the same photograph that I sent Sra. Evita Duarte
de Perón asking for help to obtain a rubber arm, but I have waited in vain
and still have not received an answer and for this motive I send this letter
certified."[19] This missive again offers clear evidence that many letters to Eva
disappeared over the years, and that it is impossible to determine how many
individuals wrote to her.

How could Eva read all the letters sent to her? According to testimonies
accumulated by Maryssa Navarro, she had a staff of female friends who
helped attend to the voluminous correspondence. Several years ago, I met an
elderly wealthy woman who had assisted Eva with the letters. Yet how many

of them could be read each week, and how could decisions be made consistently?

In a letter from Mendoza dated March 30, 1949, the sender gave Eva the file number of a form she had submitted. In this case, a notation regarding the file acknowledged that the letter had been received.[20] By 1950 both the Eva Perón Foundation and the Secretariat of Labor and Welfare had evolved a clear bureaucratic method to deal with these requests, and we shall see later how they operated a system that appeared to be personalistic, as many letters were addressed to Eva or Juan, but all of them were treated behind the scenes, by the bureaucracy.

María Clara de Otey wrote to Eva on September 9, 1949, about the possibility of receiving a pension already accorded to her husband Otto. Otto could not collect it, as he had been sentenced to prison for ten years and had served only three. María Clara explained that the prison sentence left her, a "legitimate wife," and her children without resources and that they, too, were paying for the crime. As a result, she had become a "parasitic beggar." They all lived in this "humiliating situation . . . for a crime we have not committed." Eva evidently had her office send the information on to the national Ministry of Finance, but she did not offer the woman a subsidy apart from her husband's pension.[21]

A woman from Concordia, Entre Ríos, requested a pension in February 1950. She had already written to Eva, but during the intervening period when she had received no response Lidia's husband died and left her and her eight children to fend for themselves. She was forty-three with a twenty-four-year-old son and other children as young as two years old. One of her daughters had been named María Eva, a common way to honor the First Lady. Despite her need, her 100-peso "B" pension did not come through until January 1953. One is prompted to ask why a widow with so many minor children did not deserve the "C" pension of 150 pesos.[22]

In contrast, the plight of an epileptic young man facilitated a miraculously successful petition that apparently took only a month to resolve! In fact, twenty-two-year-old Ronaldo first wrote to Eva for help in October and December of 1947; he received a response that he had to direct his petition through regular administrative channels. After two more letters to Social Assistance, the agency in charge of the pensions, he decided to write another one to the First Lady. Finally, he received a form from the Eva Perón

Foundation indicating that he had been granted an "A" pension on April 26, 1950, a month after his last letter. This particular case shows the slippery slope petitioners faced when they wrote directly to Eva. In some cases they got immediate help, and in others they were told to direct their requests to the appropriate agency. It must have been extremely confusing.[23]

Although these petitions were supposed to be submitted in applications from individuals, occasionally labor unions intervened on behalf of one of their members, Such was the case in 1949 when representatives of the Union of Workers of Various Professions (Sindicato de Obreros de Oficios Varios) wrote on behalf of Cipriano Soza, who had experienced illness in his family and found himself responsible for three minor children. The letter, addressed to Eva, commented on her generosity and goodness, anticipating that she could be of assistance. A certificate of poverty and descriptions of his living conditions with the letter note that Cipriano was forty-eight and his wife thirty-three. They lived in one room as squatters on public land in a rancho located in a lower-class neighborhood in Neuquen province with three minor children. In addition, they cared for three other minors for whom the wife received compensation. Under these circumstances, in 1950 Cipriano evidently obtained a provisional pension of 50 pesos per month, far too little to survive on, until all the paperwork had been completed. Usually people with several children received a "C" pension for 150 pesos, but the distribution of these subsidies was arbitrary. In this case, in effect, Cipriano's wife was forced to support her family by taking in children.[24]

Raimundo Reyes relied on the Salta provincial office of the Ministry of Labor and Welfare to forward the letter he wrote to Eva in December 1950. He mentioned vaguely that he found himself unable to work at a steady job and asked her for help. He also pointed out that he belonged to the Peronist Party and included his membership number. He received an "A" pension in 1951, but the rest of the paperwork has been lost, so we cannot tell what kind of situation led to his incapacity to work.[25]

Marta Catalina de Contini wrote Eva on February 2, 1950, indicating that she had sent letters to the First Lady every December since 1948 but had never received a response. Ill and without the succor that could guarantee the arrival of "daily bread," she implored Eva to help her. "I love my leaders very much, and I admire them with an Argentine heart." She asked for a pension because she could not work. Marta Catalina continued to write to Eva without a response. Finally, on June 28, the police official in charge of declaring people to be poor certified Marta Catalina and claimed that she was in great need. In the end, the national government authorized the twenty-nine-year-old woman to receive a 50-peso "A" pension.[26] Was it her age that had kept her from getting help?

A young man sent a plea to Eva from Santiago del Estero in April 1950. He called her the "mother of the humble" and hoped that she would find mercy as he told his story of misery and woe. It seems that the young man, married with five children, found himself incapacitated by a work accident that had resulted in the removal of five of his ribs. He included a picture of his back to show the extensive scarring from the operation. The young man could sign his name well and had penned the letter himself. Apparently the photograph, without accompanying documentation, was insufficient to produce the desired result. A letter to Eva did not guarantee a subsidy, as is attested by the many such incomplete files in the national archives.[27]

A woman with an unemployed and ailing husband as well as three minor children wrote a letter to Eva in 1950 in beautiful handwriting, professing her commitment to Argentine patriotism. As many other missives demonstrate, she was not alone in honoring the Argentine hero don José de San Martín.[28]

Her husband had worked for nineteen years in the Marine Ministry until he developed heart disease, and she provided documentation that he currently received medical care. She defined herself as a "mother and wife who had fallen into despair" and asked Eva for a sewing machine so that she could work at home in her profession as a seamstress. Because the foundation's archives no longer exist, we do not know if she received the sewing machine, although the entity distributed them to supplicants with great frequency. However, on the top part of her letter appears this notation: "100 peso subsidy and a sewing machine." It appears that the foundation asked her to apply for a subsidy under Perón's 1946 decree, and she subsequently filled out the paperwork that provides a wealth of information regarding her condition.

The family lived in Avellaneda, a working-class suburb south of Buenos Aires near the meat-packing plants. Their one-room flat in a boarding house had two beds and no sheets. Her husband, who had no pension, stayed at home. The social worker testified that the family often lacked food for the children and that they were absolutely desperate because the son had neither shoes nor adequate clothing and thus could not go out to work. Given the dire circumstances, barely a month passed between the letter written on June 4 and the subsidy allocation on July 13, 1950. This woman was only thirty-eight years old.

A lengthy typewritten petition arrived at the Eva Perón Foundation in June 1950 from a sixty-four-year-old widow who lived in a town in La Pampa territory. Griselda explained that she had sought help from officials at the local school cooperative to compose the letter that explained how she had labored all her life in the difficult times before Peronism, mostly as a domestic servant and laundress. With this income she had raised two children, ages sixteen and fifteen. Now she also took care of two nephews, both orphaned. While she did not have to pay for her modest lodging, her income did not cover the costs of feeding her nephews. Most likely because her older children sent her some money, Griselda received only the minimum 50-peso "A" pension.[29] Her case again illustrates how inconsistently the standards were applied.

Most of these letters came from people who had lived most of their lives in one place, or if they had immigrated to Argentina, had settled in one locality and stayed. One case showed how difficult it could be if public authorities had to locate someone who had moved. In an undated letter Enriqueta Antonini thanked Eva Perón for everything she had done to help her unnamed son. But now it was her turn, as an elderly woman living in La Plata, to ask for help. She was alone and rarely able to visit her hospitalized son. However, when officials went to visit her and verify her situation, she seemed to have moved to another locality in Mar del Plata and could not be found. Although this probably delayed the resolution of her case, it turned out that her move was only temporary, and the police learned from neighbors when to return. In January 1953 she received her pension. As no other paperwork accompanied this petition, authorities must have known the situation of both the son and the mother.[30]

Occasionally, legislators were asked to expedite the granting of a subsidy. A senator from the province of Buenos Aires wrote a note to Armando Méndez San Martín, asking him to intercede with the Eva Perón Foundation in the case initiated by Elvira Brione. Elvira asked nothing for herself, but rather for a woman who lived in Santa Fe province. The woman had a shoulder ailment and had lost the use of one arm. She often had to travel to Córdoba for treatment but found herself too poor to afford the expense, as she had lost her parents four years earlier and her siblings did not help her. We do not know what happened because only these two documents remain.[31]

A barely literate forty-two-year-old Spanish immigrant widow who had lived many years in Argentina wrote to the Eva Perón Foundation for help. She lived in Vera Jobson, in the province of Santa Fe, and had ten children ranging in age from several months to twelve years. Two children worked part time—the eldest sold vegetables and one of the daughters had employment as a babysitter. They lived together in an adobe-and-straw hut, and their income comprised the two salaries of the children. Although no formal decision appears in this file, the notation on the cover—1951/57—indicates that they received a subsidy during that time.[32]

Similarly, María del Carmen Sula, a sixty-year-old woman from rural Catamarca, resided in an adobe hut that someone had given her. There she lived with her ten-year old nephew and took in laundry. Unable to work, she asked Eva for a subsidy. María del Carmen filled out the paperwork, and the file included a note from a local authority approving the pension that was granted in September 1950.[33]

Juan Colmenar, a sixty-year-old gardener from Catamarca, was absolutely indignant when he was rejected for a subsidy that he called a pension. It seems that he had a number of grievances regarding the failure of his employer to pay him for his vacation days, as well as the government's denial of benefits that he believed he deserved. With six children, he was willing to work elsewhere, and believed he had rights as a Peronist. Therefore he wrote to Eva in February 1951 to see what she could do for him. As a result of the inquiries that were made, it emerged that Juan was originally denied a subsidy as he had received money after the federal intervention in Catamarca, but that had ended. Caseworkers suggested he be awarded a 150-peso grant, but he was eventually given a 100-peso "B" subsidy in May 1952. Perhaps the fact that he lived rent free in a house owned by an older son had led authorities to reduce the suggested subsidy.[34]

Olivia Canseco lived in Dolores, province of Buenos Aires. Her husband had abandoned her and gone off to Córdoba, leaving her with four minor children. As she explained in her petition to Eva in 1951, Olivia could barely survive, let alone provide food for her children, in whose name she requested a subsidy. The caseworker estimated that Olivia needed at least 300 pesos per month; she was paying 55 pesos for her lodging and was five months behind in her rent. This mother had been forced to sell off house furnishings to feed the children. She was not granted her "C" subsidy of 150 pesos until February 1952, and one wonders how she survived until then.[35]

Celestina Rivera, only thirty-four years old, had seven children, ages two to eighteen years old, and no husband. She begged Eva for help. Celestina lived in one room with the five youngest children and could not ask for familial aid. One of fourteen children herself, from La Pampa territory, Celestina had siblings ranging in age from sixteen to forty-six. Only one of them made a decent salary of 500 pesos per month as a police employee. Her parents were still alive, caring for the brood. Celestina worked as a laundress, for which she received a meager 13 pesos per month. The caseworker defined her morality as "mediocre," given her unmarried status, and to add to her situation Celestina was illiterate. It appears that she received a subsidy until 1960 according to notes on the cover of her file, but even 150 pesos per month, the maximum, would not have solved Celestina's problems.[36]

The Eva Perón Foundation

The last major institution established by Eva Perón in the early years of the Peronist administration proved to be her crowning achievement: the Eva Perón Foundation. She built it upon a series of caritative ventures she had begun in 1946, distributing food, clothing, work, and sewing machines. Initially she used Juan's former chauffeur, Atilio Renzi, to collect the donations and store them in an abandoned garage. "When Perón had gone to bed Evita would go down to '*las Delicias*' [the garage] with Renzi, with the Presidential cook Bartolo, and with the two footmen Sánchez and Fernández, and they would sort the merchandise, pack it up, and label it for shipment."[37]

Acknowledging the need to make her welfare plans more formal, on July 8, 1948, Eva set up the María Eva Duarte de Perón Foundation and obtained legal recognition from the government. Eventually the title of her organization was shortened to the Eva Perón Foundation. Its statutes of incorporation included provisions to provide monetary assistance and build houses for the indigent as well as building schools, hospitals, and other welfare establishments, and generally to "satisfy the basic needs for a better life of the less privileged classes."[38]

Fraser and Navarro astutely observed that the performance of legions of the poor, sick, and homeless lining up to speak to Eva could have been handled more discreetly through the use of her social workers. Eva, though, wanted that performance. "But it involved human contact that is rare in bureaucracies. These people believed that the President's wife cared about them, even loved them. In most cases, the very strictest criteria of need were summarily waived."[39] While Eva may have waived these criteria, the remaining letters, particularly those that dealt with pensions, showed that beneath Eva's compassion lay a bureaucratic welfare state.

The stories of Eva's activities at the foundation became the source of rumor, exaggeration, and class hatred. Because she kept no formal accounts, this led to fertile speculation on the part of both her supporters and detractors. Recent studies by Emilio Tenti Fanfani and Mariano Ben Plotkin have made it clear that government subsidies formed the largest percentage of contributions, followed by those of labor unions. Furthermore, trips to the foundation became a Peronist ritual that encouraged Eva's charismatic connections.[40]

While the foundation became best known for the long lines of poor people who sought personal interviews with Eva, providing the poor with a direct channel to old-age pensions became equally important. Although these petitions were supposed to go directly to the government agency in charge of old-age pensions, many people bypassed that organization to seek personal contact with Eva and her foundation. Elvira Albina from Tucumán applied in this way. While the paperwork entered the government on July 15, 1950, it came as the result of a foundation social worker's report on Elvira, which noted that the supplicant had directly communicated with Eva regarding her son and three minor children. He worked at the San Pablo sugar factory and lived in a house provided by the company. Accompanied by a letter from the Commisary of Police in San Pablo attesting to the family's need, dated September 28, 1950, as well as a certification of poverty issued on December 13, 1950, it also contained the legal form stating that Elvira was sixty-five years old and arthritic. The file does not reveal the outcome.[41]

Florencio Pitone wrote to Eva on July 26 sending "millions of wishes for happiness for the companion of our father President Perón." Once he finished with his wishes for the president and his wife, Florencio settled down to the matter of explaining that he had suffered from a skin ailment for two years, one that left him unable to work. Orphaned, he had no one to care for him, and he was hospitalized in a hospital in Córdoba province. Florencio never submitted any other paperwork, but according to a notation on the cover of the file it appears that he received a pension from 1950 until 1962.[42]

A desperate mother of ten children appealed directly to Eva for a pension because her husband's pay could not cover the family expenses. Mariana sent her best wishes to Eva, stating, "My soul has great happiness knowing that you are feeling well," and she sent her wishes as well to President Perón. This family lived in Charata, Chaco province, where the municipal hospital certified that she suffered from chronic bronchitis. A certificate of poverty, issued to be sent to the Eva Perón Foundation, affirmed the situation of the family. The petitioner obviously was poor and ill, not elderly, and she received a pension until May 1955.[43]

Some people wrote to Eva at the presidential residence, but others directed their letters to her at the Eva Perón Foundation. In August 1950 a poor laundress sent such a letter from San Juan province. She addressed her First Lady as "*Queridísima* Evita" (my dearest Evita) and explained that she had been working for thirty years as a laundress but now suffered rheumatism in her hands, which made it impossible to continue. She characterized her situation as "intolerable and in great need." Marta closed her letter again seeking a closeness with Eva by calling her queridísima, and she also sent her best to Juan. Although the rest of the paperwork is lost, the cover indicated that it had been sent to the Ministerio de Asistencia Social y Salud Pública.[44]

Bárbara Ricardo may or may not have written to Eva. No letter exists in her file. What it does contain is a supportive social worker's report dated July 9, 1950, from the Eva Perón Foundation regarding the seventy-seven-year-old whose husband abandoned her thirty years earlier. After that she had two children, at the time aged thirty-nine and twenty-four, with another man. On September 25 Miguel Naon of the División General de Asistencia Social authorized an "A" subsidy of 50 pesos for the elderly woman, one that was transmitted to her by the Eva Perón Foundation on the following day. The official paperwork did not arrive for another two years.[45]

The Women's Peronist Party, founded by Eva, also served as a conduit for petitions for old-age pensions. Rosalinda Lorenzo wote a letter on the stationery of the subdelegate of the local party office of Paso de los Libres, Corrientes, to Eva explaining that she was a seventy-nine-year-old widow with only one fifty-five-year-old daughter to help her out financially. The March 17,

1950, letter had a notation with Eva's initials: "Dr. Méndez, $50 subsidy." Evidently her wishes were honored; Rosalinda indeed received an "A" subsidy on May 3. According to the cover page, Rosalinda continued to receive the pension until 1959, indicating that Perón's overthrow by the military in 1955 did not necessarily disrupt pension benefits.[46]

Ramonda Arroyo had to wait two months for help from both Eva and her foundation, but once they acted on her request, they did so without waiting for the legal paperwork. During all this time Ramonda, a laborer, was hospitalized in Córdoba. Initially in November 1950 a delegate of her labor union, the button makers, advanced her petition and advised Eva that they had already contacted the Eva Perón Foundation without a response. Consequently the delegate asked for "your infinite goodness" to result in a favorable response. Ramonda also personally wrote to Eva at the same time from her hospital bed, indicating that she had only received a notice that she had to fill out the appropriate forms and submit them to the National Office of Social Assistance. In October Ramonda informed the secretary general of her union that she still had heard nothing and that she needed the money to purchase antibiotics and pay for an operation, yet, as of December, the Office of Social Assistance had received no paperwork from Ramonda. Finally, on December 18 Miguel Naon granted her a preliminary pension of 50 pesos per month until the paperwork arrived. This news, once again, was transmitted by the Eva Perón Foundation, not his office.[47]

The Eva Perón Foundation sometimes gave out pensions to people who simply asked for jobs. On May 2 a woman wrote from Gualeguay, Entre Ríos province, asking for a job of any type. Instead, in April, she was awarded a category "B" pension of 100 pesos per month by Naon, and she was informed directly of this news by the Eva Perón Foundation. The files regarding this decision have been lost, so it is impossible to analyze why a pension became a better prospect than a job.[48]

Constanzo Resifra obtained help from the Eva Perón Foundation on September 22 without prior paperwork. Eva had signed an approval for a 100-peso monthly subsidy (type "B") and signed the slip herself. On January 5, 1951, a social worker had interviewed him in Buenos Aires province. The forty-two-year-old Italian pastry cook lived with his thirty-one-year-old wife (who had problems with her arm) and five minor children. He also lived with his elderly father who had no old-age pension and whose brothers helped out because Constanzo had been disabled since September 1949. They all resided in one room of a wood-and-tin house and rented out the other rooms. The family already owed a grocery store more than 1,000 pesos. Constanzo must have contacted Eva earlier, but the paperwork has been lost.[49]

Gerónima Leto, a sixty-four-year-old illiterate widow who lived in La Pampa, sent a letter through intermediaries "with her faith placed in the Dama de la Esperanza." She related how she had worked all her life, the last twenty-eight years of which had been as a widow. She had worked as a domestic servant, a day laborer, and a laundress, and now she still needed income to help raise two grandchildren, ages twelve and nine, after having raised three children of her own.[50]

> I have dedicated my entire life to my grandchildren. It is my greatest
> disappointment to be unable to complete my mission to raise and educate
> them with the product of my labor. But I have confidence that with the
> aid of the Fundación María Eva Duarte de Perón I shall be able to achieve
> my tasks and end my days blessing the cause of General Perón and the
> soul of his companion "Evita."

Not only Gerónima but the justice of the peace who signed her certification of poverty believed that the help would come directly from the Eva Perón Foundation, even though she placed her thumbprint on paperwork from the Dirección General de Asistencia Social in February 1951. And the following August she received an "A" pension of 50 pesos per month.

Another widow, Paulina Raíces, lost her husband at sea during a terrible storm in September 1948 along the coast of Patagonia and didn't even have the solace of being able to bury him in a cementery. Paulina was left with a young son; only the local priest had been able to find work for her to support the two of them. Thus she wrote to Eva on January 16, 1950, asking for financial help. By April 24, once again without having received all the legal paperwork, Miguel Naon cut through the red tape and authorized an "A" pension for Paulina. Two days later a note from the Eva Perón Foundation informed Paulina of this decision. Subsequently local officials were informed that Paulina had written to the First Lady, and she asked them to send the necessary information to the Dirección de Ayuda Integral—that is, the Eva Perón Foundation—instead of the Dirección Nacional de Asistencia Social, which was in charge of awarding subsidies.[51]

Over and over people wrote to the Eva Perón Foundation, and those with urgent needs received aid before filling out the paperwork. All of them, however, conformed to the law and submitted the paperwork after having received the pension. This rapid processing seems to have been the only advantage of writing to the foundation, as people in very similar situations who applied through the regular channels after 1950 had their petitions granted after complying with the law. The large bulk of surviving petitions, whether directly to Eva or to the Ministerio de Trabajo y Previsión, date from 1950, and administrators must have been absolutely swamped by the daily arrival of administrative paperwork once the availability of these pensions became more well known. Up until that point people relied as much on family connections as on religious institutions and mutual-aid societies, the very organizations that the welfare state wanted to replace.[52] Many immigrants and Argentines were reaching the end of their productive years, some sooner than imagined due to misfortunes, and often because of abandonment by a spouse. Illness also took its toll.

The people who appealed to Eva's generosity usually did not have access to the welfare systems in the capital city. Most lived in rural areas, were elderly, and had few contacts with the political world. These were precisely those people for whom the bureaucratic safety nets often failed, and they also rarely migrated from rural areas to cities. Thus, on the one hand they were extremely poor, but on the other they were well known enough to get the paperwork necessary to receive the paltry sums offered by the pensions.

The Infirm

A great many files contain only fragments. One such case comes from a small town in the province of Córdoba. The illiterate petitioner, Paulino Vásquez, informed Eva that he was a widower with two ill children. One, the eldest son, was paralyzed and could only survive by sitting up on a chair. The other seemed to be mentally challenged and under treatment. Paulino himself walked with a limp and could not find work. A notation on the file indicated that Paulino would need someone to fill in all the necessary paperwork in order to receive a pension, but it is unclear whether this happened.[53]

Almost all the petitions regarding illness that do not relate to age or to family needs came from men. Andrés Soto, a Chilean, arrived as a bachelor from Chile in 1932 and made his way to Quilmes, a city in Buenos Aires province. Evidently he did work initially, but he eventually began to suffer from a lung disease that completely debilitated him. In June 1951 he sent Eva a letter in care of the Eva Perón Foundation, asking for help. The caseworker discovered that Andrés had been in and out of hospitals for his lung condition and had no relatives in Argentina to care for him. Homeless, he resided in a municipal shelter in downtown Buenos Aires. He ended up in the hospital again but did receive a subsidy, which he held until 1960. As an immigrant, Andrés benefited from the same forms of social welfare enjoyed by a citizen.[54]

Aldo Romero, fifty-eight, suffered from mental illness as well as a heart condition. Completely unable to work, he wrote Eva from his hospital bed in Bahía Blanca, province of Buenos Aires, in October 1951. Single and a day laborer, Aldo could neither pay his bills nor support himself. From a notation on the cover, Aldo received a subsidy until 1958.[55]

A baker from Córdoba had the bad luck to fall ill from inhaling flour dust as he worked. A bachelor, he had no one to care for him as his sister resided in Buenos Aires and had a family of her own to care for. For this reason, in September 1950 he wrote to Eva asking for a monthly pension until "God and the Virgin call upon me." He suffered from bronchial asthma as well as a gastric ulcer, and he was granted an "A" pension in April 1951. It is unclear how he expected to care for himself and find shelter with absolutely no help.[56]

José Jesús Comaro, from a village in Santa Fe province, also asked for an old-age subsidy. A bachelor, he was fifty-nine when he applied, and he had spent his life as a lumberjack (hachero). Illiterate, he asked a policeman to write to Eva for help. He lived with a poor niece who had four children. Despite his absolute poverty, the fact that he could depend on his niece, according to the caseworker, changed his poverty from "absolute" to "relative." In spite of this downgrading of his poverty, José Jesús obtained a subsidy that he collected until it was cancelled in 1957.[57]

By 1951 requests for subsidies seem to have been channeled completely through the Eva Perón Foundation. Employees of the foundation helped people get the certificates of poverty that they needed. The foundation provided the caseworkers to aid the applicants in filling out the questionnaire and also rendered judgments on a case-by-case basis. This meant that the sustained functioning of the subsidy relied on the continued good health of the foundation's head, something that could not be guaranteed. By 1951 Eva's health was jeopardized by uterine cancer. Indeed, 1951 marked the end of the files on these subsidies located in the national archive. There do exist files that contain lists of files purged later on the grounds that they were expired (*caducado*). These types of files increased in number after the military coup that overthrew Perón in 1955, but they began to appear before that time period. This meant either that President Perón, who took over control of the Eva Perón Foundation, wanted to end this haphazard subsidy, or that government officials began to check files for people who had died. In any case, this convoluted experiment in aid for Argentina's poor, especially those living outside of Buenos Aires, had come to an end.

What becomes clear from studying this process is that people wanted to bypass the bureaucracy when asking for help. The arbitrary designations of pension awards meant that the 1946 decree failed miserably to provide an organized welfare system. Like the other people who could apply for the subsidy, those with families, while grateful for what they received, must have wondered why the system seemed more like a thicket of obstacles rather than justice for the poor. Thus, people felt far more comfortable reaching out to Juan and especially to Eva. They needed to have someone listen to their stories, empathize with their dilemmas, and provide loving relief. The letters, long buried, bear witness to the melodramas of the rural Peronist poor. And even if the subsidies amounted to pittances, they are proof that the powerful sometimes listened to the homeless and infirm. The personalized process of seeking and allocating subsidies through Eva's foundation offered a kind of dignity not present in earlier modes of charity. The charismatic connection between Eva—and to a lesser extent Juan—and the needy kept the aloof and indifferent bureaucracy at bay, at least for a while.

CHAPTER 3

Pent-up Needs

Juan's Plan de Gobierno

ARGENTINE CITIZENS, BOTH rural and urban, had pent-up consumer, social, and health needs. For countries involved in World War II, consumer demands had taken second place to the war effort. In Argentina a desire for a better life resulted from other factors. The impact of declining world prices for grains and beef during the Depression, increased migration of poor Argentines to Buenos Aires in search of work, and the toll that these events placed on families and communities became a crisis by the 1940s. Not only did migrants see the difference between the way they had lived in the countryside compared to the better standards of living promised to organized urban workers by Juan Perón, those who remained at home found themselves bereft of family and community support and far from the consumer and health benefits offered by the new democratic government. Provincial governments had little to offer those left on the farms and ranches, while migrants turned to new sources of beneficence coming from Eva and her transit homes and from Perón's government.[1]

Juan Perón's recognition of the loyal support he could garner by encouraging Argentines to write directly to him (or Eva) infused another of his political strategies. While chapters 1 and 2 deal with letters initiated by the people and directed to Juan and Eva, this chapter focuses on a very different set of communications initiated by invitation of Juan Perón. Perhaps the president had an instinctive feeling that people needed to connect with political leaders and their parties or, after having worked on projects such as disaster relief for the 1944 San Juan earthquake, he understood the long-standing frustrations that people had toward government officials.[2]

In any case, in December 1946 the newly elected president undertook a mass-media campaign designed to incorporate public suggestions into government programs (although on a far more modest scale than the one he would launch in 1951). The number of letters, their sophisticated suggestions, and the general literacy of the population laid bare, as had the earlier private correspondence, a crying need for change, especially in the countryside.

Perón consolidated various pieces of legislation already introduced by the executive branch into his first five-year plan, the Government Plan (Plan de Gobierno), to reorganize and modernize government. All types of laws, including female suffrage, fell under the scope of the plan, and implementing it meant clarifying the role of the state in social welfare.

To deal with the many needs Argentines faced, the president aimed to set a clear leadership path. Perón's Plan de Gobierno provided means to accomplish this but, unlike his second five-year plan in 1951, little has been written about this one, even though it constituted a major symbolic invitation for the masses to feel connected directly to Juan.[3] The plan itself eventually comprised approximately 130 pages of programs. It included twenty-seven already-proposed laws reorganizing all the ministries, providing new regulations for the federal capital, reforming education, restructuring the foreign service, instituting new norms for social welfare, and creating electoral rights for women and members of the military. Clear charts accompanied each proposal to document the need for change as well as the resources available to accomplish them. The plan included no timetable for changes, nor did it specify which projects would be implemented first or where they were to be located.[4]

The absence of specific goals for all communities can be explained in part by Perón's desire to rationalize government and reform the bureaucracy. To announce his plans, the newly inaugurated president gave a press conference on September 30, 1946. He observed, "Previous administrations have left us nothing, absolutely nothing that constitutes a *national* orientation for us to carry out."[5] He blamed part of the problem on the absence of an entity under executive control dedicated to technical issues, a situation that had enabled financial interests to dominate state policies. The president intended to rectify this by creating a Ministry of Technical Matters (Ministerio de

Asuntos Técnicos) and to implement a plan of government with the twenty-seven laws. Before that, however, he wanted to make these proposals known to the Argentine public, from the industrialists to the illiterate. Once Perón received feedback from these groups, he would be willing to discuss the Plan de Gobierno 1947–1951.

The Plan de Gobierno included female suffrage, customs reforms and energy laws, and plans for public construction. The charts that followed the proposed legislation offer the easiest way to see what kinds of priorities were assigned to different economic, social, and political themes. For example, despite the breadth of the legislation under the rubric of school construction, the government planned to construct only thirty-seven buildings divided among primary and secondary schools, teachers' colleges, and schools of commerce. As the buildings were located mostly outside the province of Buenos Aires, the migrant population would not necessarily be served, but it might keep others from undertaking the taxing journey to Buenos Aires. The same was true for the forty-five projects divided among different types of trade schools. Only six university buildings were planned, distributed among Buenos Aires city and province, as well as Córdoba, Santa Fe, and Entre Ríos provinces. The document listed only three hydroelectric facilities to be initiated in 1947, followed by fourteen in 1948, ten in 1949, and so on. These could not be built near the national capital, where demand for electric power was highest, because no rivers flowed there, and engineers had not yet developed the technology to transport electricity over long distances. The Plan de Gobierno—along with ideas for reforming administration, building dams, and promoting irrigation—in many ways represented the hopes of Peronism, rather than the reality. The lack of specifics actually encouraged people to write letters demanding more details.[6]

After announcing the plan, Perón convened a press conference to discuss the components of his government reforms on October 1, 1947, but only spoke specifically about public health. He then ended the press conference due to the late hour and reconvened it on October 2, when he introduced the topics of education, justice, foreign relations, national defense, the economy, immigration, and labor. He devoted only a few minutes to each, as seen in the written transcript. Two days later Perón held another news conference in which he presented issues related to transportation, public works, architecture, roads, public transport, national parks and tourism, mining, fishing, industrialization, commerce, finances, budgets, and taxes. Some topics merited several paragraphs, others one sentence. Nevertheless, it appeared that the president wanted to stake out positions on just about everything political, social, or economic.[7]

Later, in October 1947, he spoke to workers at a meeting of the powerful General Confederation of Labor, organized to endorse the five-year plan. There he intimated to the attendees that his government profoundly supported workers' causes. He envisioned the plan as a great source of employment for workers, to benefit and protect the weak. This probably created anxieties among middle-class and professional groups that wanted to influence Perón. For people who had no government or military pensions and were wary of the government plans, the anti-Peronist newspaper *La Nación* further stirred the criticisms by arguing that the plan intended to end other pensions and fold them into the government's social-security plan. Nevertheless, the paper faithfully reported positive comments on the plan.[8]

On November 17, 1947, the *New York Times* published an article on the five-year plan with the headline "Five Year Plan Gives Full Power to Perón. Argentine President Will Become Head of System of State Socialism." In it the author, clearly no fan of Peronism, particularly objected to the proposed military expenditures, presidential oversight of school construction, and socialized medicine.[9] The author's fears had little to do with what really happened on the ground because, despite the increase in revenues from the foodstuffs sold to European nations during World War II, Perón simply was not in any position to undertake comprehensive measures to solve all of Argentina's problems.

National and international objections coincided with Peronist plans to build a new Argentina. As in the case of the pension plan, many petitioners were referred to appropriate agencies while, at other times, the requests were too personal or of too little interest to the new government. These obstacles, however, did not deter people from writing, and they expected responses. They even sent Perón books to read. María de Gorman sent a book her husband had written called *Veinte años perdidos* (Twenty Lost Years) and asked for an interview with the president. She had written the letter "with the conviction that the time has ended when our supplications by correspondence were thrown into the trash basket before they were placed in the hands of those who governed." Unfortunately for this petitioner, she received a letter back telling her that the president was too busy to schedule a meeting with her, but at least she had the satisfaction that someone in the government had taken notice of her husband's book.[10] Eventually Juan relied on Eva to meet with the people in scheduled and unscheduled interviews. President Perón issued a very specific invitation to make policy suggestions, an idea that was totally different from the passive acceptance of personal missives that had been sent to the presidential couple before this time. Nevertheless, people had been thinking about policy reforms even before the official invitation.

National Recommendations

Early on, the government received an anonymous plan for land reform that addressed rural needs. The writer believed that land-tenure problems were due neither to landowners of large properties nor to the condition of the labor force. Although he did not oppose foreign landownership, he wanted farmers to receive the bulk of agricultural profits. To accomplish this, the anonymous writer suggested a return to an Argentine tradition from Bernardino Rivadavia's early liberal government of the 1820s. At that time the government of the province of Buenos Aires expropriated lands not privately held and rented them out through emphyteusis, a system of land rentals at low prices. The idea of an Argentine remedy rather than one based on the ideology of a foreign country proved particularly attractive to the Perón government, since it defined itself as a nationalist regime, and it was suggested that emphyteusis "should be consulted as an antecedent at an opportune moment." In many ways this rural plan paralleled the idea of massive government construction of urban apartments. As the writer put it, "Land will end up in the hands of those who work it." In this fifteen-page document, the unknown citizen acknowledged the dangers of state intervention and argued that agrarian reform should be implemented within prudent limits.[11]

Rural inhabitants seemed particularly anxious to communicate with the president. Perón received a letter, also written in June 1946, from a tenant farmer (*colono*) worried about the sons of other farmers:

I am a son of this land, an Argentine married with four children, aged fifty-two. I am a tenant farmer of the Tenant Farmers' Institute [Instituto de Colonos] of the province of Buenos Aires, a *criollo* [native-born] who honors our race. I have struggled for many years in obscurity and anonymity, and have risen from the status of a peón making 20 pesos per month, to the point where I am free of landlords. . . .

I want you to know that neither I nor my sons need land because I have enough to live on for now. But in the future a farming family with many children like us in the countryside will end up with a *minifundio* [a property with too little land to support a family], or we will lose our livelihoods. These children of tenant farmers are raised in the difficult struggle of the countryside and almost illiterate. . . . Today General Perón leads all the needy and Argentina shall be greater and less selfish.[12]

The author of this missive offered himself as a consultant on rural matters in Argentina, and informed the president that he had sent along written plans for the creation of a model agricultural colony in Buenos Aires. He echoed the belief of others that before Perón could change the realities of Argentina he needed to find out about farming, and letter writing served this purpose.

On June 27, 1946, Eliana de Aros Romana suggested new legislation to the president to train and certify domestic servants so that they could obtain work more easily. In this case Eliana, a midwife and Red Cross nurse, had an extensive record of interacting with poor women. Furthermore, she had met Juan earlier in Córdoba province:

In October 1944, as secretary of Labor and Welfare, you were invited to a demonstration of sympathy in Villa María (Córdoba province). I attended as President of the Córdoba Association of Midwives. . . . During the trip, I conversed with several of our group about the situation of domestic servants and I explained my plan and promised to present it. I did submit it to the Intervener of the Córdoba Region, Captain H. Russo, who enthusiastically endorsed it. Even though I tried several times to talk to Col. Mercante [Domingo Mercante, eventually Governor of Buenos Aires province, editor of the pro-labor newspaper *El Laborista*, and one-time candidate for Peronist vice president], I could not obtain an audience.[13]

Undeterred, Eliana wrote to the new president. Along with her letter, she sent her preliminary legal proposal (*preproyecto*). Her plan would require a series of qualifying documents—including an identity card, a certification of conduct, a certification of good health, and a certification of competence (*idoneidad*)—that women could use to improve their chances of finding work. With these papers, Eliana believed women could find work, even in the interior. As women migrated with ever-greater frequency to the capital city, it became increasingly difficult to obtain reliable domestic service in the provinces. Eliana defended education for poor women as a way to satisfy the domestic-service needs of middle-class women. However, such training would not guarantee higher wages and thus could not solve the problems of poor women from the interior. From my perspective, such correspondence clearly demonstrated the author's middle-class concerns about the dwindling supply of domestic servants.

Some ordinary citizens responded immediately to Juan Perón's call for their opinions. On October 27, 1946, Roberto Desnate set down his thoughts, noting that he had changed party affiliations to become a Peronist:

In my modest condition as an Argentine citizen, lover of justice, equality, and all those initiatives and actions that have as their goal the common good of men, I cannot silence the intimate spiritual satisfaction that such ideas signify.

The five-year plan that your excellency outlined before the honorable chamber of deputies should not only make an impact within the nation and the world, but also awaken a new consciousness within us. That will permit us to advance within the strict guidelines of justice and to construct together our great Patria, until yesterday asleep, having been muzzled by bad politics and self-interests that since colonial times have benefited the few and prejudiced the many.

We have systems of scaffolding completely unsuitable to current conditions; these inadequate structures signify dismal consequences for humanity. For this reason, I cannot conceive how an Argentine can remain indifferent or resigned to this great endeavor recommended by your excellency and whose benefits will lead to a better future. . . .

I long served the healthy principles of Yrigoyenism [the followers of Hipólito Yrigoyen], devoid of personal partisanship, until I became embittered by evil caudillos. Then I opted to join the Laborist Party, section one [predecessor to the Peronist Justicialista Party] and I am now one of the general secretaries of an affiliate. I have never held a political office and despite the fact that I need to support my wife and five children, nobody can say that I have taken advantage of a special situation, or bothered anyone. I continue to collaborate anonymously because I understand that it is the duty of all well-intentioned men.[14]

Less than a month after the October 1946 Desnate letter, a Spanish immigrant wrote to Juan on November 28, effusively characterizing the plan as "simply great" and "wonderful." "No one who is not a knave or an idiot would oppose this work." Turning to the question of land reform, he suggested establishing more agricultural zones to protect lands against urban encroachment.

When the war broke out in 1914, accompanied by disaster, in many areas ranchers bought up leagues of land near the towns, suffocating them. The sharecroppers had to leave in search of cheap land; some moved as far as 600 km from Buenos Aires, and thus began the horror. Agriculture . . . would enable Argentina to compete in international markets throughout the world.[15]

Equally important, he claimed that zones like La Pampa, farther away from the coastal area, produced more and better beef (although he provided no statistics). He explained that his knowledge of the land derived from forty-two years of residency in Argentina and from having raised sixteen children. He had remained in the countryside until the 1937 drought killed all his cattle, forcing him to make his way to the city, not attracted to its "lights" as some of who he called "shameless writers" stated, but in "search of work."

News of the invitation to write to the president spread quickly throughout the country. In December 1946 three people—two women and a man—urged the president to include an institute for mental hygiene as part of the twenty-seven laws to be folded into the five-year plan. Shortly thereafter, on December 4, 1946, Perón received another letter from a small town in the province of Tucumán where two sisters eagerly offered to work for the plan during their vacation time:

We, the writers of this letter, María C. and Pilar Alonso, native

Argentines, unmarried, twenty-seven and twenty years old, live in the town of San Miguel, Aguilares, Tucumán. One of us directs National School 280 and the other teaches at the National School 55 in Tucumán. We respectfully understand the enormous importance of the incomparable plan in fomenting the prominence of our patria. Aware of this it is our great honor to write to you, your excellency, offering our services in the months of January and February (vacation months) so that we can humbly contribute to the goals of the plan.

At the same time, we will forego our salaries for those vacation months by returning to our parents' humble abode, built for nine children. This way we can reduce our household expenses during the vacation period.

We would be happy to go wherever you think it necessary. We await your orders and you and your wife are in our prayers.[16]

This altruism, if Perón read the letter, must have cheered the president. No documentation accompanied the letter, and no evidence exists that the Secretariat of Technical Affairs created by Perón had devised a way to answer such correspondence.

The Argentine Union of Intellectual Workers in Buenos Aires wanted the government to establish new political schools designed to teach the basic principles of the five-year plan as they related to history, geography, and civics. And then to further justify this endeavor, they included suggestions on several other topics. The petition, signed by the head of the union, affirmed that its members supported the national aims of the plan.[17]

A Mr. A. Baroni originally sent his ideas for the plan to the military secretary of the presidential residence because he was the brother-in-law of a military man and his son had been a cadet at the military academy. His introductory note was accompanied by an extensive report dated February 1947, which began, "Directions and suggestions from a Juniano [one who supported the military coup of June 1943 that overthrew Pres. Castillo] who didn't believe in the 'shirtless ones.'" Baroni now recognized the president as a "statesman capable of producing such an unlikely movement." The president, he predicted, "would ultimately share with the Great Captain (José de San Martín, the illustrious Liberator of South America) the precious title of 'LIBERATOR.'" Eighteen pages of suggestions followed this effusive praise.

Baroni sent his plans to several government officials and, as a result, several copies remain.[18]

Hernán Costa Zapata wrote to the chief executive on November 25, 1946, informing him that he had already written several times. On this occasion he wished to demonstrate his solidarity with the Plan Quinquenal, as the Plan de Gobierno was now called. He had heard Perón speak at the Colón Theater and experienced deep "moral and spiritual satisfaction." He hoped that God would assist Perón and his followers in implementing the plan. Costa Zapata's own contribution consisted of a proposal to promote irrigation systems in Argentina that he believed could increase agricultural profits by 1,800 percent. Once again rural issues motivated this correspondence.[19]

In this same vein, Eduardo Dante, a Frenchman who had migrated to Argentina in 1889, wanted a better life for his sons who had served in the military. Eduardo complained about the fate of farmers exploited by merchants who purchased their crops at disadvantageous prices. He wrote from Entre Ríos province hoping that the president would clarify and strengthen the rights of farmers in the plan.[20] An Italian immigrant wrote to the presidential residence in December 1947. The letter, written in Italian (with an official translation into Spanish), began with a holiday greeting to the first family. Dante went on to announce that he was a journalist who had developed three proposals to deal with industrialization. He concluded by offering the plans with no expectation of personal reward.[21]

A Spanish industrialist wrote to Juan from Onteniente, asking that the plan incorporate provisions for the construction of a textile factory. If this were to happen, the petitioner would move to Argentina with his son who could operate the factory. He included a poem:

President Perón: A Sonnet
A new sun rises impetuously, illuminates with an intense strength,
And brings forth healthy fruits of a better and more harmonious future

This boundless rising sun helps bring fertility to the valley below
With all its virtues

A new Hercules crosses another road,
Transforming the fate of the country from sadness to happiness.

With his just work, he brings the urgent desire for peace among men,
Today a model, and an allegory for the future.[22]

This proposal, clearly reflecting the personal desire of a Spaniard to immigrate to Argentina with a promise of an industrial job for his son, did not elicit a sympathetic response. The five-year plan was intended to benefit residents of Argentina, not future immigrants.

Regional, Provincial, and Personal Proposals

On June 5, 1946, a man sent a memorandum to the president suggesting construction of one hundred thousand apartments of various sizes to be rented for 20 pesos per room for twelve years. Thereafter renters would become owners. He also suggested fifty thousand apartments with slightly higher rents, but with the same prospects of ownership. The author then boldly recommended that they be constructed in a newly founded city on the outskirts of Buenos Aires to be called Ciudad Perón. Notations on this document tell us that the letter so interested the government that on July 16 the plan was sent to the Department of Labor and Social Welfare for consideration. At that point in time, however, the government had no institutional entities capable of dealing with such a provocative idea.[23]

The following day, the president of the Cane Cutters' Center of Tucumán (Centro Cañero de Tucumán) in northwest Argentina conveyed hopes that the government would sustain higher sugar-cane prices. He did so in the belief that the organization of sugar laborers by the Peronist Party meant that agricultural workers would finally enjoy some of the benefits this regional industry had brought to the northwestern province. The letter was sent to both President Perón and the head of the newly created Ministerio de Asuntos Técnicos.

> I write to you and through you to your commission in charge of studying
> the sugar industry . . . suggesting how to reach a stable solution by fixing
> the sale price of sugar to reflect the shared costs of all parties, and by
> raising the salaries of hundreds of thousands of workers who participate
> in various aspects of the production and processing of sugar. In our
> note of May 23 we wrote that the president of the national Central Bank,

don Miguel Miranda, maintained that it would not be a good economic idea to hike the pay for those who plant sugarcane, nor for the worker, especially if the economic future of the province were jeopardized by paying more for sugar, which already costs more than price obtained in the market.

This proposition (according to cane cutters) seems to be founded in the desire to protect the consumer, one that has been expressed by the national press and by politicians during the many years that the Saveedra Lama Law (which determined how to calculate sugar prices) has been in place—since 1912. The sugar consumer ends up being the spoiled child of high sugar prices, because he pays three times more for other foodstuffs that utilize sugar.

This is the crux of the problem: people of Buenos Aires believe that to protect an industry means to help out a group of privileged individuals— the sugar factory owners and large sugar cane landholders, and it is in the North that we suffer the effects of that belief that keeps us in poverty, to benefit the black marketeers and the producers of sweets who rely on sugar as a main ingredient.[24]

The president of this association knew that Perón needed the support of the cane cutters. He also realized that any increase in the price of sugar could lead to accusations of price fixing, so the problem was complicated. Furthermore, under the Yrigoyen government, consumers had often been better protected than rural workers. He argued, however, that under Peronism "when the Argentine consumers learn that sugar prices have risen officially, in order to support these important social benefits, they will pay it with pride."

The petition of cane growers underscored the regional issues that long divided Argentina, as well as the reality that the interests of urban consumers (as well as landowners and sugar manufacturers) often trumped the needs of rural workers. It showed rural cane growers to be acutely aware of the political history of sugar production, not surprisingly more so than the president. Thus they had to educate the national government regarding the realities of the Northwest and how much Peronism needed the support of the working class there.

Several notations appear on this petition. First an undated memorandum from the Directorate of Economics, Finances, and Statistics to the Secretaría

Técnica (another name for the Ministry of Technical Affairs) argued that it would be important to know the complete history of sugar prices and sent the document on to the president of the Central Bank. Another note emphasized how important it had been for the association to explain the political economy of sugar. And a letter written in June 1946 showed that the matter was still being discussed.

School construction also appeared as a significant concern of letter writers. Soon after Perón assumed office, a group of residents from Resistencia (Chaco territory) sent him an extraordinarily well-thought-out plan to construct a school in their area. It included maps of the proposed location, along with an extensive and detailed justification for the school's construction. In this letter, they addressed the president as *Excelentísimo compatriota* (Most Excellent Compatriot).[25] The school project, like the many that would be submitted to Perón for his second five-year plan (Segundo Plan Quinquenal) in 1951, represented the desires of groups of rural folks, mostly poor. This letter also conveyed the concern that rural dwellers would be bypassed as the cities grew and this translated to even more outmigration. Perhaps the school would enable remaining children to find jobs in the provincial and national bureaucracies.

A sergeant major organized his rural neighborhood in San Juan province to put together a plan in response to Juan's request and sent him a letter on November 7, 1946. Not only did they have ideas, they wanted to invite the president for dinner to chat with him about them. The soldier felt that the proposal would be difficult to implement, but he and his neighbors were convinced that General Juan D. Perón could deal with "the holocaust of the working class in the country, no matter what it cost," and they believed that the desire for collective improvement superseded individual needs. They interpreted that "the Plan's principal hypothesis to destroy the avarice and speculation that causes hunger and create a new social conscience based on justice and the law." However, he and his group wanted to see more concrete measures that would achieve this goal, and he described the situation as "life and death." The suggestions they offered included the construction of more schools, especially trade schools, to prepare future citizens. The need for schools in the interior was a leitmotif in the correspondence from Argentines living outside Buenos Aires, but this letter offered a glimpse of group desperation rarely seen.[26]

Gino Lucca wrote to the president on November 22, 1946, to tell the leader of his interest in improved colonization and immigration schemes. This writer had evidently seen the widespread depopulation of regions in the interior, and he identified himself as an "old and well-versed person regarding the interior of the country." While he applauded what the president had included in his Plan de Gobierno, Gino also produced a document called the Colonia Modelo General Perón designed to further colonization schemes in the province of Corrientes, a place of particular interest to the author. He called it a colonia to indicate it was a new settlement, this time dedicated to the native-born, rather than the immigrants who had filled up the colonias in the nineteenth century.[27]

On December 14, 1946, a group of teachers from Rosario, Santa Fe, wrote to Perón about a bill under consideration by the congress to pay student teachers, noting that

> the Five-Year Plan proposes perfecting what exists and creating what does not exist. Permit me to make a comparison between a teacher of the province of Santa Fe and a national one. First of all, I believe there is a proposal to start the pay for provincial teachers at 200 pesos (per month), followed by a scaled increment of 30 pesos every five years; that is to say that after twenty-five years of work one would earn 300 pesos. National teachers start out at 350. I don't know if this is the same for all provincial teachers. . . .
>
> I have always believed, Sr. President, animated by a profound spirit of justice and patriotism . . . that the pay scale should be the same for a humble provincial teacher [as for a national teacher]. I know that you support this deep in your magnanimous, wholesome and unpretentious heart.[28]

The problems of social security coverage also preoccupied those who sent suggestions to the president. Accordingly, in October 1946 the officers of the Real Estate Auctioneers Center (Centro de Martilleros de Hacienda y Bienes Raíces) wrote asking to be included in any social-security plan through the establishment of their own pension fund. They had been trying to get a congressional law passed since 1938, and they had spoken to Vice President Ramón Castillo in 1940. As they put it, "The right to life is an obligation that the State must support from the moment of a person's first breath until Destiny separates him from the world; anything else will be 'unpardonable.'" It is unclear how they linked individual to corporate rights, and little came of their petition.[29]

Only a few newspapers dared to critique the Plan de Gobierno. Indeed, all through October and November of 1946, the major newspapers simply cited aspects of the plan as well as professional meetings held on the subject. On December 3, 1946, *La Prensa*, no fan of the president, published a critique of the plan offered by the Argentine Chamber of Commerce and sent to the national congress. The group criticized the demanding residential requirements for those who wanted to enter the country to work and critiqued the idea that workers should eventually receive shares in the companies that employed them. Furthermore the group suggested the elimination of special pension funds for public employees in favor of a more equitable and universal system of social security as well as the power of the president to arbitrarily raise duties on particular imported items of national interest.[30]

On December 11 *La Prensa* reported on a meeting of youth. They complained that Perón's plan, which had never meant to be totally inclusive, left out the issue of land redistribution in small plots to farmers so that the countryside could benefit from the postwar economic boom. Migration statistics seem to indicate that people in rural areas preferred to respond by moving rather than wait for such recommendations to be included.[31] Generally speaking, the objections to the plan remained muted, while new demands outside the limits of the Plan de Gobierno emerged.

Suggestions for Constitutional Reforms

Once the president opened the doors to ideas for improving Argentina, recommendations for constitutional reforms appeared among the suggestions. In November 1948 a Spaniard residing in Bahía Blanca wrote that he had lost his land to fraud and had heard of many others who lost theirs due to bankruptcy. He wanted a constitutional law to guarantee that relatives within the sixth degree could inherit land. After that, no one could take it away from them, even if there were liens on the property. That same month, a representative of the Argentine Agrarian Federation in Buenos Aires province reported abuses he had seen in the countryside: large landholders intimidated smaller farmers, blocking off roads to the smaller holdings and making it difficult for children to attend school.[32] Pablo Garena of Posadas suggested a series of constitutional reforms including equal pay for women and minors, worker control of the economy, and the elimination of the anti-anarchist measure called the Residence Law passed in 1902 to deport activist foreigners, a law he called derisively the "the Oligarch's Law" (Ley de Oligarquía). His letter was countersigned by many *amas de casa* (housewives).[33]

Given the anti-anarchist tradition in Argentina, it was difficult to reform the general immigration laws. Undeterred, a justice of the peace from Buenos Aires wrote to Eva on October 29, 1948, asking for his letter to be passed on to Juan. He wanted the state to promote immigration of refugee children to Argentina where they would receive automatic citizenship. He had in mind children accompanied by their parents, but he also wanted orphans who would be placed with foster parents under the custody of the state until they were eighteen. He suggested the elimination of all legal distinctions between children born of married parents and those who were declared illegitimate under several categories. This issue related to inheritance laws, but the legal discrimination also placed public stigma on children born outside of wedlock.[34]

This judicial official's approach to child immigration was very well intentioned, but it eventually conflicted with anti-immigrant and especially anti-Semitic efforts to prevent the immigration of refugee children. Nonetheless, his interest in the elimination of legal categories of illegitimacy became part of Peronist law in 1948, along with more flexible adoption laws and a new statute to create legal equality between legitimate and illegitimate children. Thus the judge's suggestions, with the exception of child-immigration laws, soon became the law in Argentina without a constitutional amendment.[35]

In 1948 the Peronist government triumphantly published *Perón cumple su Plan de Gobierno* (Perón Fulfills His Government Plan). Twenty months after its implementation, the government declared it a great success and claimed it had accomplished even more than original official estimates. In terms of its social politics, the pamphlet declared that social policies could be divided into two eras—Before Perón and After Perón.[36] The advent of Peronism had humanized the city and the countryside, improved wages, and promoted social justice. In other areas, the government declared it had exceeded expectations. New laws forbade the public revelation of a child's birth status—whether born inside or outside marriage. A new University Law had been passed, which made education free and opened it to women, and new schools had been opened throughout the country.[37]

The Argentine Socialist Party strongly objected to the self-congratulatory proclamations of the Peronists, accusing the government of fomenting spiraling inflation. Policies that inflated salaries, increased pensions, and raised prices, along with the purchase of many industrial plants from foreign owners, had led to an 81 percent decrease in foreign exchange available to the government. Moreover, problems such as the shortage of fossil fuels had been ignored.[38]

From an Argentine historiographical perspective, Norberto Galasso and others have described the first Plan Quinquenal as principally designed to organize government activities in a way that emphasized national liberation and social justice.[39] More recently Patricia Berrotarán has argued that the plan, for the first time, "instituted and informed these new norms not only for the state, but also society."[40] Although she did not consult the letters written by people in favor of the plan, they clearly affirm her point of view. This chapter has demonstrated that the functioning of the Plan de Gobierno was directly linked to the lines of communication that opened up between the government and the general public. The letters demonstrated that people believed the new president would listen to their suggestions, and that it was optimistic to think about a better Argentina after years of quasi-military rule. In contrast, those who wrote letters to enhance their own situation tended to meet with disinterest.

The early official efforts to promote correspondence between citizens and the president paved the way for the construction of charismatic ties between Argentines and Juan Perón and his administration, at the same time that the president's wife, María Eva Duarte de Perón, cultivated her own charismatic relationships. The first five-year plan provided a path for communication between the government and the people that did not rely solely on political parties. However, Juan Perón had never intended to make the ties reciprocal. He wanted the people to write but felt no obligation to respond. Nonetheless, the perception that the president listened to their problems and heeded their suggestions had begun to take root, in no small measure reinforced by the efforts of Eva to bond with the people. Taken as a whole, the two-way channels of communication promoted a fictive closeness that surpassed the one-way "fireside" chats utilized by President Franklin Roosevelt and subsequent US presidents. In those cases the presidents invited the public to listen, but not to be heard.[41]

The letters we have examined in this chapter represent the beginning of what people perceived as a mandate to communicate with the president. They flooded the presidential residence, the Ministry of Technical Affairs, and the offices of political officials close to Juan and Eva. They came handwritten and typed. Some arrived in the form of telegrams, some on official stationery, and others on scraps of paper. The deluge had begun. Many letter writers seemed to have formed associations to put through their group suggestions, while a few wrote to Juan about their own problems, instead of seeing the larger picture. In 2004 Omar Acha suggested that Argentine citizens formed many new associations not directly associated with the Peronist Party, ones that never would have been organized before the elections of 1946. He, too, based his article on letters from the Secretaría de Asuntos Técnicos that dealt with other topics. The letters regarding the groups that wrote to promote the first five-year plan reaffirm this hypothesis.[42]

However, it was one thing to have people write letters to national leaders, and quite another to have national leaders who designed plans to encourage letter writing. When Juan Perón took office on June 4, 1946, both his enemies and supporters had expected major changes within Argentine politics. Perón did not disappoint either side, but his new approach to charismatic populist politics frightened many—from the organized workers who beleaguered the president in Buenos Aires to elites who wanted no part of an organized system of social justice.[43]

Without doubt, more letters exist that refer specifically to the Plan Quinquenal, but they remain hidden in the haphazard filing of the overall correspondence that addresses this plan and the subsequent one put forth in 1951 (covered in chapter 4), mingled together in the same boxes. The reality of both correspondence campaigns, however, underlines the fact that Perón invited the people to write after his agencies had already drawn up the plans. This meant that it was either a cynical move on Perón's part, or that he perceived that governmental legitimacy rested upon the perceptions of communication and exchanges of ideas. However, the letters also reveal that people wrote to Eva and Juan before the announcement of the Plan de Gobierno. The perception that the president would listen to their suggestions accompanied the people's enthusiasm about the building of a new nation under Peronism. The letters go beyond personal melodramas in expressing collective aspirations for the nation, the province, or particular professional or interest groups. President Perón had tapped into a deep well of opinions and good will, even among the poorest of the nation's inhabitants.

CHAPTER 4

Reaffirming the Charismatic Bond

The Segundo Plan Quinquenal

ON DECEMBER 3, 1951, Juan Perón announced plans to launch a second five-year plan. He began by reiterating that he was shocked, upon becoming president, to find that Argentina had no organization designed to promote planning. And despite the modest goals printed in the first Plan Quinquenal, the president claimed to have achieved infinitely more than what the first plan had considered the minimum targets. Indeed, he boasted that seventy-six thousand ideas had been implemented, and that the plan's content dedicated to "economic independence, social justice, and political sovereignty" had been achieved. Furthermore, the plan had ended the long history of politicians turning to congress to execute their pet projects, a practice eschewed by Peronists, according to the president. Instead, technical commissions responsible to the executive branch had consulted with groups from across the country, particularly workers but even individuals, in order to discover "lo que el pueblo argentino necesita" (what the Argentine people need).[1]

No matter how rosy a picture the government painted of Argentina's economic progress during the first five-year plan, the country's reconstruction was plagued by regional and sectoral demands for the limited resources offered by the Peronist government. Inflation, a postwar phenomenon in Europe and the United States as well, led workers and consumers to protest, while industrialists and the agricultural sector had their own complaints. For example, farmers could not sell their crops at international rates but only at much lower prices established by an Argentine government agency, the Argentine Institute for the Promotion of Trade. The government thus ensured that agricultural production would finance industrial development. By 1948 the annual inflation rate hit 30 percent; it increased even more the following year, despite government efforts to reduce the amount of currency and credit in circulation. Government policies thereafter favored export agriculture over domestic industry to improve the balance of trade, but inflation continued to increase. The second five-year plan should have been ready for implementation by December 1951, but poor economic conditions resulted in postponement until 1953.[2] The extensive proposal was written in January 1952, six months before Eva's death, and it represented the type of popular project envisioned by Juan and revealed the instrumentality of charisma to its success. The death of the First Lady and the absence of a charismatic personality soon challenged the success of new Peronist plans.[3]

To reinforce the charismatic overtures embodied in the first five-year plan, the president envisioned a far more coordinated effort of letter writing. Thus he asked for more consultation and wanted people to write to him before December 31, 1952. According to Eduardo Elena, "approximately 42,000 pieces of correspondence" arrived at the Ministry of Technical Subjects, the entity Perón had organized earlier to formulate consistent state policies for all sectors of the economy. Elena has examined how this letter-writing campaign dealt with public works and fit into Perón's efforts to end price gouging and control the consumer economy. Natalia Milanesio expanded on this topic to focus on female consumers, but to date no one has linked this campaign to other Peronist letter-writing efforts and social issues.[4]

The invitation to write to the president, taken up by so many people, represented perhaps the most ambitious effort by any populist government to reinforce charismatic connections. Although the plan did not begin until 1953, by 1955 when the military overthrew Perón, letters littered the Ministry of Technical Subjects. Just as in the case of the letters directed earlier to Eva, it is impossible to distinguish between correspondence sent directly to the president and those that went to the ministry. Yet it is clear that countless Argentines from all walks of life wrote to Juan about everything from the sublime to the ridiculous, including fantastical inventions. This chapter examines this correspondence, much of which has been organized in the Argentine national archives under the headings of "Social Matters," "Inventions," and "Education."[5]

The second five-year plan, over five hundred pages long, proposed general projects but did not outline specific tasks or timetables. Thus Perón's request for feedback inspired wide-ranging responses from those who took advantage of the newly opened path of direct communication to offer suggestions. Juan reinforced this sense of participation by sending groups of experts all over the country to assess local and national needs. Comments on the files reveal that planners considered some suggestions that came from the letters, had already included some suggested by experts, and rejected others as beyond the scope of their authority or impracticable. In a few cases, notations on the file covers branded the authors as simply crazy.

The letters addressing the Segundo Plan Quinquenal were, on the whole, less far-reaching in their proposals and more limited to local scenarios. The ebullience and nationalism evident in 1946 had waned in the face of inflation and other economic problems that seemed to be less easily resolved. Furthermore, Eva's death factored heavily into the responses, as we shall see.

Argentina without Eva

As the extent of Eva Perón's illness became clear, the president and his advisers must have become concerned about how to maintain charismatic connections to the people. Shortly after she fainted in January 1950, the First Lady underwent an operation for "appendicitis." Doctors, as was customary in 1950s Argentina, never revealed to her the exact nature of her illness. To maintain secrecy, she received radiation treatments to control bleeding, again without her knowledge. Indeed, she never even knew that the physician who operated on her for the second time for cervical cancer in 1951 was an American, Dr. George Pack. The last person she saw before receiving anesthesia was her Argentine doctor, because she had often expressed her aversion to North Americans. On August 31 Eva renounced her intention to seek the vice presidency alongside her husband. At that time she did not mention her illness, but rather she expressed her desire to continue working with the Peronist Parties, both male and female. Nor did she address the military opposition to her candidacy.[6] However, in his radio chat of November 3 Juan acknowledged his wife's illness and stated that he had suspended all partisan political activities to be by her side.[7] When Pack operated on Eva three days later, the surgeon discovered the cancer had already spread to other organs.[8] Thereafter she seemed to waste away; by the time Perón was elected for a second time, his wife had to be held up with a metal scaffolding and covered with a fur coat to appear at the inauguration.

By early 1952 Eva's condition became obvious to many people. One man wrote to the Ministry of Technical Matters asking the state to subsidize his trip to France so that he could pray for Eva's recovery. He planned to travel to New York by the Pan-American Highway, and make his way to Lourdes by plane and hired car. The ministry ignored this proposal.[9]

Peronism had to prepare for a political world without Eva's participation. Her decision in August not to run for the vice presidency was due as much to her declining health as to political opposition. Thereafter she appeared in public much less frequently, often without Perón. What would Peronism do without the "bridge of love" she had forged between Juan and el pueblo?[10] As Maryssa Navarro poignantly notes, "'In every real sense,' Perón wrote of the years 1950 and 1951, 'I had lost my wife. . . . We saw each other only occasionally and then only very briefly, as if we lived in different cities. . . .' In Buenos Aires, she foiled by small deceits Perón's attempts to make her eat regularly, and fooled the president by working all night and arriving in time for breakfast."[11]

During her last months, Eva reputedly worked on a manuscript entitled *Mi mensaje* (My Message). Her last will and testament formed part of the manuscript, and a typed fragment of part of the document with her initials has been recovered. The full will was read publicly by Juan on October 17, 1952. Significantly for this book, in it Eva announced, "I would also wish that the poor, the elderly, the children, my *descamisados* [shirtless ones] would continue to write me as they do in these times of my life."[12] This aspect of her will was fulfilled.

On February 8, 1954, Sra. Paquiano, a migrant from Santiago, wrote to Eva from Tapiales, a small town in the province of Buenos Aires, begging her to keep the children at the Martín Rodríguez School. She began writing to Eva in 1949 about her two children, Hernán and Humberto, aged ten and thirteen at the time, and requested that they be placed in a school because her husband made too little to support them and their two older brothers. Eva had taken a special interest in these children. Furthermore, she had awarded furniture to the family. Heeding Eva's testament, Sra. Paquiano thought that she could reach the First Lady beyond the grave, although the request proved fruitless.[13]

The loss of Eva on July 26, 1952, weighed heavily on many Argentines who wrote to Juan. Almost two weeks of official mourning accompanied the movement of poor people by trains, buses, and cars into Buenos Aires so that all could pass by her body, which was exhibited publicly and then given to Dr. Pedro Ara, a famed Spanish mortician, for further treatment. After Juan was overthrown by the military in 1955, the new leaders so feared that a religious cult would develop around the worship of her body that they stole it. It was secretly shipped to Italy, where it remained interred in a cemetery under a false name until the 1970s when, after Juan's death in July 1974, it was returned to Argentina for burial.[14]

One man answered the call for comments on the second five-year plan by commenting on Eva's death:

President: your beloved spouse and constant companion has entered into immortality; the country has lost its most beloved daughter; it has lost its *alma tutelar* [the peoples' guardian]. She gave pieces of her life to the humble, the children, the elderly, and finally to those submerged for so many years in slavery and misery by the oligarchy. Her multiple works formed by her own hands throughout the country provide proof of Evita's moral context. She was unsurpassed in her social action, clearly the greatest woman in the contemporary world.[15]

To honor her memory, José Cano suggested in a letter sent to the Ministry of Technical Affairs on October 20, 1952, that "all public employees who feel uncomfortable under Perón should resign within thirty days." He also urged Juan to take over the Fundación Eva Perón, a piece of advice the president took to heart, except that he proceeded to reduce it in size and scope.

In 1954 young Mercedes Noemí Reynals, a first-grade student, wrote in *Mundo Peronista*, "You were the only woman who offered her white hands to the needy and handicapped." She further identified Evita as the good fairy and a mother to all Argentine children. This magazine was published until Juan Perón was overthrown in 1955 and often contained letters from children idolizing both Juan and Eva.[16]

Eva's popularity should not be underestimated. An entire book filled with poems and songs dedicated to Juan and Eva appeared in 1966. The great majority had been written to elevate Eva on a Peronist pedestal from which

no one could dislodge her. Significantly, the book, written in the midst of
strong opposition to Peronism and at a time when Eva's body still remained
secreted in an unmarked grave in Italy, demonstrated the depth of positive
emotions evoked by Eva's name. It also invoked the melancholy of the tango
as well as an increased intolerance for the middle and upper classes.[17]

Guillermo Pérez, who wanted a plan to protect people from traffic acci-
dents, wrote his proposal on paper emblazoned with pictures of Juan and
Eva. His statements also included the sentiment that only the workers
embodied true Peronism.[18]

National Plans

While people remembered and revered Eva, they were less sanguine about
the prospects of major improvements in the new Argentina. In letters regarding the second plan, national complaints did not reflect the eternal optimism
seen in 1946. For example, Miguel Eloisa of Lomas de Zamora, Buenos Aires
province, wrote a long letter to the president on December 4, 1951, criticizing
the corruption of municipal and provincial governments. He griped that
citizens paid taxes for services they never received. For this reason Miguel
wanted the president to nationalize local services to ensure that citizens were
not defrauded. What he insisted upon was that there be no "state of divorce"
between the desires of the national government and local authorities. He
invoked language usually associated with Eva to reinforce his suggestions by
claiming that the president should exercise "poder tutelar que tiende a pro-
teger la gran familia Argentina" (tutelary power to protect the great Argentine family). He also complained about the inadequate education students
received in schools and universities that inhibited the government's ability
to achieve its goals. What he wanted, in effect, was a strong authoritarian
executive, something rejected by Perón during his first presidency.[19]

Carlos Briano also became very excited by Juan's invitation to make suggestions for the next Peronist administration. His suggestions implicitly criticized existing low wages for domestic servants, as well as Juan's old-age
pension and subsidy plan. The very day after Perón's radio speech, Carlos
wrote a letter suggesting a fund be created to give domestic servants a 250-
peso per month pension for women over fifty and men over fifty-five—a sum
much higher than the pensions given to the poor and needy and reflective of

how inflation affected the poor. "To cover the costs, employers would pay an additional ten percent of the salary and the servants the other ten percent, that is, 20 percent of the minimum salary." The fund could begin to operate five years later. The file did not include a response. His suggestion was followed a week later by one from Rosario, Santa Fe, suggesting that housewives receive a pension. Elena Dacosta wrote as a Justicialista and Peronista that such a gesture would be typical of the president.[20]

Some Peronists complained that the fixed paid annual vacation law should reflect the number of years of service. For example, Carlos Gianini of Buenos Aires wrote on January 14, 1952 (after the cutoff date suggested by the president), that people who worked for twenty years should receive an entire month of paid vacation, while others who had worked fewer years would accrue fewer vacation days. Furthermore, if a worker took another job, his vacation pay should be cumulative. He finished his letter, "I do not doubt that my humble suggestion will be received as a modest collaboration . . . in this Justicialista hour created by the government of the revolution and well fulfilled by your excellency."[21] Such verbose and flowery language often appeared in these letters.

A worker from La Plata, province of Buenos Aires, believed that President Perón was "capable of transforming the political, social and economic panorama of the country" (thereby repeating what Perón had said on December 3) and wanted to collaborate with the president from a perspective that had no "ideological tendency," as he did not belong to any political party. Peronism and the Segundo Plan Quinquenal should focus on providing work for all adults and education for the young. To keep Argentine youths striving to work in productive jobs, he also urged that the government ban their attendance at theaters, restaurants, and any other recreation that might prevent them from reaching their goals. To accomplish this, he suggested the formation of a ministry of work "that would control all the tasks that each person should accomplish, each according to his ability." This worker again reflected fascist tendencies that often appeared among Peronists. Nevertheless, the plan did include programs for workers' apprenticeships.[22]

One man, Arsenio Felippa, identified himself as a "humble pensioner." He lived in the Buenos Aires suburb of Avellaneda and defined the fight against capitalism as one of the interests of Peronism. To counter capitalism, he suggested the elimination of land auctions, which he believed to be antidemocratic, as well as sales, outside major cities, of small lots of land. "It is my humble opinion that in our dear patria, at least [the ownership of] land should be within the reach of the poorest workers. . . . What do you think of this plan? Suppress auctions of land, and in their place, establish a lottery advertised by notaries?"[23]

After the new year, a pharmacist wrote to Juan to reiterate the contents of the letter he had sent in January 1950 to the Eva Perón Foundation in which he offered to contribute to the foundation 50 pesos per month. In 1950 the contribution was intended to honor the Year of the Liberator General San Martín. Now he wanted the January 1952 sum to be used for "the stimulation, development, execution, etc. of initiatives or suggestions approved or it can be transferred to the Eva Perón Foundation fund." In response to his request for the review of his unusual offer, officials noted on the file that it had been returned by the Ministry of Work and Welfare "because it was not within the competency of this ministry." So the idealistic pharmacist's letters most likely remained unread by the president and his First Lady, but his clear support offers testimony to the charismatic nature of the Peróns, especially Eva.[24]

Grand economic plans—past, present, and future—seemed to elude the people who still wrote to Juan and Eva regarding social issues. Many, particularly those living outside the city of Buenos Aires, were too old or infirm to work, and some had been driven off their lands by droughts and other agricultural catastrophes. Now they wanted new schools and factories for rural areas to keep them in their homelands. This type of personal correspondence continued to pour in to Eva and her foundation but did not conform to Juan's request for solutions to larger problems.

Several writers, all men, urged Perón to make divorce legal as part of the second five-year plan. In a letter of December 4 Marco Lura argued that the lack of a comprehensive divorce law was the result of "the ineptitude of previous governments." Marco had other suggestions regarding the sanitary disposal of waste and the creation of an honor tribunal where workers could complain about the lack of hygiene in their places of work—as if honor equated to cleanliness. Two days later Eduardo Saletti weighed in on the matter of divorce as well, requesting

an adequate and humane divorce law that could be allowed, once only, to repair errors and justified motives, but without falling into prostitution like what has happened in the United States. If one begins to study this issue, it is almost inevitably linked to first marriages that for obvious reasons of youth, end in separation with rare exceptions for those with children and without a law that can legally repair situations created by fatality, leaving children destitute, sentenced to an existence that is amoral and abnormal for society. For the rest of their lives, and even more ridiculous, Argentine law is inferior to those of other countries, even where people divorce several times, and where they are helped by the Law.[25]

Although Perón did not include divorce in the plan, he did decree a divorce law in 1955, six months before he was overthrown by the military.

Regional, Local, and Personal Plans

On December 7, 1951, Ricardo Fuentes wrote to President Perón invoking Eva's interest in children's homes. He lived in the city of La Plata, where the Ciudad Infantil Armanda Allen had been constructed by the Eva Perón Foundation. Ricardo suggested that in line with that project, a city for the elderly should also be built with the same enthusiasm. Although the letter was sent to the appropriate agency, no additional information indicated whether the government wanted to build such an entity. Eva's death probably deterred this project.[26]

Less than two weeks after Perón made his radio announcement requesting written suggestions, a letter came in from a labor union in Corrientes regarding four construction proposals for the region, including a school, a hospital, a bridge, and workers' homes. Bureaucratic notations indicated that the new school, designed for the existing seven hundred students, had been included already in the second five-year plan. The other projects had not. Furthermore, a 1954 note indicated that the local bank did not believe the bridge proposal warranted funding, so only part of the Corrientes petition was funded.[27]

People wanted schools so badly that neighbors pitched in to purchase an old building in Entre Ríos province so that the government would rank the rehabilitation of the building much higher. In their letter of December 21, 1951, residents of Pueblo Cazés told their story:

We the neighbors of the locality of Pueblo Cazés and Colonia San Antonio of Colón . . . write to his excellency, General Juan Domingo

Perón to explain that this neighborhood has an urgent problem that has existed for many years without favorable solution, and paying attention to your radio speech of the third of this month, related to the second five-year plan, we respectfully make the following petition:

(1) In Colonia San Antonio . . . National School 118 has functioned in a privately owned property of the Jewish Colonization Association. (2) This building because of its age is in a very bad state and in danger of collapsing, and thus it is totally inappropriate for the function for which it is used. (3) The school is 2,000 meters from the village that is Pueblo Cazés and the students from that town comprise the majority. (4) The JCA has donated land in this location for the construction of a new National School 118. (5) The neighborhood has pitched in by acquiring the building offered by the Ministry of Education of the Nation [presumably the old one].[28]

Many inhabitants of both towns signed the petition. Evidently the specialists collecting data for the Segundo Plan Quinquenal had already scheduled the construction, as seen in the notations on the file. Another petition to Juan came from Sauce Norte, El Tala, Entre Ríos, written five days later, asking only for the addition of classrooms. This, too, had already been included in the plans.[29]

A union of rural workers in Santiago del Estero, in northern Argentina, made a similar case for school construction in their neighborhood. Someone had donated the property for the school, which had been accepted by the government. They also wanted a well drilled along with an irrigation canal that would secure the future of the community that had been founded in 1700, but now had grown and required new infrastructure. Indeed, the population had burgeoned with the founding of a small school in 1912. Several classrooms had been added on, but the petitioners believed that a new school should be built as soon as possible. Along with the other works, the residents believed that such measures "were the only hope for our present and for the future of our children." A subsequent note in the file mentioned the plan had included only the school construction.[30] These and other initiatives explained in letters to the Peronist government clearly indicate that people did not always expect a simple handout for projects important to their communities.

Indeed, many of the school requests arrived complete with blueprints, records of land or building donations, and extensive petitions. Equally important, their vision was local, not national.

Economic matters as well as schools weighed heavily on rural folk. Just after the president invited the pueblo to write to him about the second five-year plan, on December 9, 1951, a tenant dairy farmer from Sarandí, located near the city of Buenos Aires, wrote to Juan.

> I am responding to your call to Argentine workers to write to you, as a worker whose only plan is that people listen to you. And to know that you receive this letter soon means that my dreams will be converted into a reality, and so should it be. You, who have done so much good for our country; you who have favored all the Argentine workers, make me realize now that your efforts to favor all the workers from this day forward, have not yet favored the dairy farmers.

The dairy farmer went on to say that he had to express some 400 liters of milk to make ends meet because the cost of so many other basic consumer items like *alpargatas* (rope-soled canvas shoes)—which went from 3.80 to 5 pesos—had gone up.

> Our employer . . . owner of almost 200 hectares and I don't know how many animals, makes us live in a miserable hut with one dormitory and another room where our children sleep which has no plaster for walls, nor a bath. Now that you ask for our collaboration in the Segundo Plan Quinquenal, here you have our case and we dairy employees await your response.

The request was acknowledged with a note stating that committees of experts would study such problems.[31]

Santa Fe provincial deputy Nazareno Rossi sent a petition signed by farmers from the San Jenaro district of his province, all of whom hoped that land reform would occur during the following five years. They wanted the president to forbid the eviction of any tenant farmers, stabilize the prices of the land, and have prices that were reasonable. They asked for a ceiling of 2.5 percent interest to make payments within reach of landless tenant farmers. More than thirty-six tenant farmers signed the petition. These people still aspired to be landowners.[32]

For people who had taken out mortgages on their homes, the thought of losing their main source of security from foreclosure or eviction was very frightening, especially as inflation began to take a toll in postwar Argentina. On January 23, 1952, Adelina Garza from Córdoba wrote the president to urge him to protect homes from seizure, for whatever reason. She wanted a new slogan: "now in the New Peronist Argentina no one should be without their humble home, but rather that they should feel pride in calling it 'my house.' I profoundly feel this way because that is how I feel about my own idea."[33] Many people benefited from the incorporation of that philosophy into Peronism, as it became impossible to evict tenants or seize homes.

Lorenza Donatti addressed her letter to Juan with the title "Mi Problema" (My problem) and told him that she was about to be evicted by the mortgage bank from the house she had lived in and rented for the past twenty years. Despite her shock about what had happened, she remained calm because she knew that Perón as a father would take care of her. Her letter, bound with other assorted papers, was not accompanied by any paperwork relevant to her case.[34]

Early letters supporting the second five-year plan thus urged Perón to revise the rental statutes as well as mortgage and land sale laws. One came from a landlord who wanted to dislodge one of his nonpaying tenants. The owner identified himself as a member of the local Peronist Party. To help his case he invoked the name of Evita and claimed to be a former railroad employee as well as a descamisado, a "shirtless one." This petitioner, however, now had shirts and property, an indication of how much the working class had benefited during the early years of Peronism.[35]

A second Peronist landlord reaffirmed the frustration of property owners who could not dislodge their tenants. Manuel Fuerte, who lived in the countryside near the city of La Plata, sent the president paperwork regarding the long time it took the courts to deliver verdicts on rental cases—specifically ones that affected him. After all, his tenant had paid no rent since 1947. Manuel, himself a professional working in the municipality of La Plata, listed the names of many prominent Peronists who supported his case.[36]

On February 1, 1952, police employees of the territory of Misiones wrote to the Ministry of Technical Subjects asking that a million-peso subsidy be tacked on the plan. The "immediate" goal of the group was the construction of a health clinic, a social center, and a sports field. No plans indicated the costs of these works or the projects that would encompass the rest of the million pesos. This project was sent on to another department.[37]

In April 1952 one petitioner wrote to Juan Perón for an audience concerning various plans that he sent to the president. Osvaldo Martínez worried about the ability of newlyweds to purchase their first home. To help them, Martínez suggested that a state agency should obtain property in Gran Buenos Aires (the neighborhoods that surrounded the Federal District) to construct homes, all of which would be similar, and distribute them through a lottery operated by the Eva Perón Foundation. Oscar suggested that the homes could be made of prefabricated materials and reassembled on site.[38]

The inflation that threatened homeowners and renters also affected consumers, and some letters requested a freeze on prices for subsistence goods. One suggestion linked this policy to a fixed salary scale for all workers in Argentina that would limit the extreme variations found in many working-class professions. These suggestions, written on stationery from the Peronist Party in Córdoba on December 27 and signed by the general secretary of a *unidad básica* (local affiliate), expressed great hopes that the president would heed his suggestions. This was just one of several letters written by this author on the same day to the president that called for such disparate items as the construction of cemeteries and laws to moralize the country, including a ban on reading novels.[39]

While the labor leader from Córdoba hoped that the president might read his words (no response seems to have been forthcoming), another wanted to make sure his suggestions meant something to the president and to the Ministry of Technical Affairs. To accomplish this, Ramón Aguilla made sure the readers of his suggestions knew that he was a loyal Peronist. To that end he noted that on June 5, 1951, as a "Peronist, labor unionist and Argentine," he had sent proposals "motivated by his intense desire to collaborate with the electoral campaign" and that he understood that all Argentines "had the sacred duty to collaborate with General Perón and his companion Evita." In this petition he proposed a new amnesty law for all men who had deserted or failed to serve their required military service. Had he not completed his military service?[40]

Elvira Ottone wrote to Eva Perón as well as to the Ministry of Technical Matters in March 1952 to explain her desperate situation. Eleven members of her family lived in a tiny apartment with two bedrooms, a bath, and kitchen. These eleven people in fact consisted of two married couples and their children, all encamped in a mother-in-law's apartment. "Every day the problem grows along with that of the six children and we have no solution. My husband works in telecommunications, but from a financial point of view, it is impossible to buy a home. With the hope, faith and security that you will listen to me, you with your goodness, which you have made known so many times in the name of the well-being of the working class, we ask that you provide us with something." She then quoted the president that the only privileged ones in Argentina were the children.[41]

Women treated unfairly at work also wanted equal rights built into the second plan. Perón had already given women the vote in 1947, and now some working-class women wanted more. Those employed at the US-owned Swift Meatpacking Plant petitioned to receive benefits that were similar to their male counterparts:

1. Make this a Justicialista [original name of the Peronist Party] law: Equal Salary for Equal Work.
2. Reform the pension law for women so that they can get a half pension after fifteen years of work without an age minimum.
3. Reform the Maternity Law 11.933 so that women are paid the three months' salary according to current salary scales.[42]

Their idea contrasted sharply with a December 1951 suggestion that came from another woman, who proposed a totally different tactic for female teachers. She argued that married women should have the right to retire early so that they could properly care for their families. This woman, a teacher, believed that she had particular burdens that kept her from her family. She believed that factory workers simply left at the end of the day, never had to work overtime, and had their time free for family work. Apparently she did not realize that many women labored in piecework systems where they sewed at home and received their income based only on what they produced. Her observations betrayed her middle-class views. As she put it:

A schoolteacher has many school tasks that she takes home and spends three or four hours of daily dedication and when the teacher is a mother, in addition to running the home, she has to use hours late at night to work, while the children sleep, for household activities. When the children reach the age of nine and older, it is an age of transition, so delicate and when they have so much contact with the world outside the home, it is precisely at this time that mothers should accentuate their influence. In this struggle without rest she is doubly challenged (and the mother is essential for the home and life).

When the mother ends her work in the office or factory at a fixed hour, she rejoins the family and her children completely and can attend to her tasks. When the hour of rest arrives for all, it is also for her and the next day before leaving for work, she can pay attention to the children until the last moment in order to take care of everything. In contrast, the teacher has to also pay attention to school matters at home, and this double or triple task places her in an inferior position with respect to other workers and wears her out more quickly. For nine years (out of fifteen) I have thought about this type of struggle, which needs a solution for the mother who teaches, especially when one thinks of how impotent she is when she must deal with so many delicate promises. I do not doubt the Justicialist Argentina will resolve the problem, and that the "mother teacher" problem will have a solution.

Your Excellency, I ask you to add this to all the works of justice you perform: ALLOW "TEACHING MOTHERS" TO VOLUNTARILY RETIRE AFTER SEVENTEEN YEARS OF SERVICE, WITHOUT AGE RESTRICTIONS, WITH THEIR LAST SALARY AS RETIREMENT PAY.[43]

This suggestion went to the Department of Education where it did not meet a supportive response. Prudencio Toledo wrote back, "As an ideal all mothers should take care of their children and home. . . . As far as school is concerned, it is not so satisfactory because one would lose school teachers at their moment of physical and intellectual maturity. For the State, this would be a burden difficult to overcome."[44]

The tendency of immigrants to stay in Buenos Aires concerned Juan Luna, who lived in a comfortable suburb of Buenos Aires. He believed that these settlers were responsible for rising prices, the scarcity of housing, and the increased demand for clothing. Therefore, as part of the Segundo Plan

Quinquenal, Juan wanted all immigrants, before they arrived in Argentina, to promise to live for no less than three years in an interior province, no closer than 100 kilometers to a city, a regulation he claimed existed in the United States. He believed that such a law would distribute the population more evenly in Argentina and prevent shortages in potable water, essential foods, transportation, and housing.[45]

Ideally, Perón had envisioned a letter-writing process that would take a few weeks and come to a timely end by early 1952. Notwithstanding, the Argentine public felt the need to make their wishes known to the president even after the Segundo Plan Quinquenal had been published, and writers continued to bombard the president and the ministry with letters.

A singularly persistent group of widows decided to write to the president in search of homes built to their specifications. Calling themselves *pobres vergonzantes* (the shameful poor), they requested that housing be included in the five-year plan. To relieve their poverty, they proposed the construction of homes with a bedroom, kitchen, and bath for those without family, along with small family homes with several bedrooms. Furthermore, they wanted no men involved in directing their lives. They also said they would honor the memory of Eva, who had recently died, for the rest of their lives. Fourteen widows from the capital city and the province of Buenos Aires signed this petition to the president in December 1952.

The leader of the group continued to write petitions and involved other government officials in the effort. In May 1954, after receiving yet another petition, the presidential residence inquired whether this request could be granted. Despite the continued efforts of this collective, no direct assistance ensued. This would have been an ideal project for Eva and her foundation, but she had died, and Juan Perón lacked the savvy to deal with the issue.[46]

Another group of people tried to get Juan to include a construction plan for an old-age home in Mendoza province. In a letter addressed directly to the president, the Committee to Defend the Rights of the Elderly claimed that Mendoza needed "a home, a city, to house its numerous elderly people to alleviate their physical problems, the sadness of their souls abandoned to indifference and injustice." Some received 100 pesos per month from a provincial pension, but that was not enough even to feed themselves. In response to this request, the government of Mendoza claimed to have a program to construct a home for the elderly and wisely suggested that it be operated by the Eva Perón Foundation. The files do not indicate whether the home was constructed or whether the national government participated in funding.

Inventions and the Imagination

Included in the extensive paper trail of personal communications is a story of a fantastical invention. On April 6, 1953, a young married woman named María wrote to the president asking forgiveness for having robbed him of his "very precious time" to present the invention of her twenty-seven-year-old husband. He spent all his spare time working on an *avión submarino* or, as he called it, a *submarplano*, a submarine that could fly. His problem was that he had no place to set it up, as the owner of their apartment refused to let him work there and finally forced him to move. To add to their problems, María had fallen ill and she asked the president if he had friends who could help her out. It is no wonder that they were not allowed to work on the project in the apartment in the city of Buenos Aires. In a second note of April 14, María sought additional consideration for another invention, the *avión torpedero* (torpedo plane). Her husband hoped to collaborate in the president's "patriotic mission" through the production of this plane that could be manufactured in Argentina.[47]

An engineer from the National Directorate of Scientific and Technical Investigations (Dirección Nacional de Investigaciones Científicas y Técnicas) answered María on May 11 and invited her husband to speak to him at any time. The rapid response indicated the degree of governmental interest in such an invention. María's husband indeed went to see the engineer and then was referred to the military division of the national directorate. Unfortunately we have no information regarding how the military evaluated this proposal, but we do know that such machines even as late as the 1970s only appeared in Hollywood's James Bond movies and that the picture that accompanied the letters looked like a child's drawing with almost no scientific measurements or explanations.

Some inventors insisted on meeting the president to provide more details on their proposals. One man, a naturalized Italian living in Formosa, had a plan to extract alcohol from a vegetable substance that would offer a new source of combustion. In his letter he mentioned that his plant could provide 37 percent of its weight in liquid fuel, much greater than that of corn, but he refused to reveal which plant provided such results. Eventually, bureaucrats washed their hands of the matter since they could not obtain adequate information to relay back to the president.[48]

Alfonso Garza claimed to have an invention that would seed clouds to produce rain. This proposal was so interesting that, as in the case of the inventor of the submarine plane, Alfonso was invited to speak with officials at the National Directorate of Scientific and Technical Investigations. Thrilled at this response, he followed up on February 3, 1953, with a letter written in downtown Buenos Aires that provided more, but not enough, details on how to seed the clouds. However, he did disclose that previous efforts had been failures. Alfonso subsequently invited the president to take a helicopter ride with him to appreciate the wonders of nature and how it could be manipulated. Such a discovery would make the president another Christopher Columbus. Unfortunately, the more Alfonso waxed poetic about nature, the more he appeared to be slightly mad. Finally, on May 19 the secretariat informed him that his theories lacked scientific proof.[49]

Samuel Ciano wrote a series of flowery, verbose letters to the president beginning on November 4, 1952, and continuing on through 1953. He contrived to get an interview with Juan to explain his unnamed inventions through effusive praise that included a homage to Eva as the "Martyr of the Workers." In October 1953 Samuel wrote once more, lamenting his inability to gain access to the president. This time he added a footnote indicating that under no circumstances would he meet with anyone else. Finally the ministry responded on December 1, 1953, that Samuel would have to be specific about his inventions before any interviews were accorded.[50]

Automobiles also had a magical significance for many Argentines. The local automobile industry was in its infancy during the first Perón administration. An Italian firm, Automotores Argentino, built a factory near Buenos Aires in 1949, producing mostly small vans. Mercedes-Benz also began operations that year to manufacture commercial vehicles and taxicabs. By the time Perón was overthrown in 1955, the company had turned out six thousand vehicles. During the last years of the Peronist administration, Henry Kaiser set up a joint venture to produce automobiles, something not really achieved until after 1955 when the factory was built in Córdoba province. Automobiles and trucks proved to be an elusive commodity during this period because there were few imports to meet the demand. Thus it is no wonder that people wrote to Perón as part of the Segundo Plan Quinquenal with suggestions about automobile production as well as requests for gifts of cars.[51]

On April 30, 1952, the presidential secretariat forwarded a file to the Ministry of Technical Affairs regarding a bricklayer from the town of Pergamino who wanted to build cars. The letter actually came from a local journalist, Zeno Román, who believed that municipal authorities were far too slow to see the wisdom of supporting local industry, having callously ignored all the noble efforts of this poor worker to make a new and powerful Argentina. Zeno sent along a newspaper clipping about the car (most likely penned by himself) that explained that the parts had been cobbled together from many older imported vehicles. He also sent a photograph and a letter from the bricklayer who had built the car. In many ways this auto foretold the future of cannibalized cars in places like Cuba after 1959 that remained closed to the import of new cars.

Around the same time, the bricklayer's wife, Marta, asked the president to meet with her husband, the proud inventor. The response from the director of the National Directorate of Technical Investigations (Dirección Nacional de Investigaciones Técnicas), however, was less than enthusiastic since the car offered no new features and only merited consideration because of "the perseverance and enthusiasm of the person who built it." He left to the discretion of the president whether to receive Leonardo, the inventor. In fact, the ministry official offered to meet with Marta the next time she went to Buenos Aires but did not recommend a personal audience with the president.[52]

Many who submitted their ideas and designs wanted more than anything else to present their ideas personally to the president. In reality, they hoped they could transform Juan into a male Eva. Luis Ramírez wrote to Juan Perón on January 15, 1952, informing the president that he had invented an emergency door for automobiles. The typical response to these interview requests involved an invitation to meet with specialists from the appropriate government agency. In this case, the secretary of the National Directorate of Technical Investigations issued the invitation and Ramírez accepted but declined to provide specific plans, probably fearing that he would lose proprietary rights to his invention without a patent. His reluctance to provide documentation, however, did not guarantee a meeting with the president, and the government terminated contact with Ramírez.[53]

Saturnino Robles believed he could control flying saucers and also wanted to meet with the president to discuss the issue because of its international ramifications. As with Ramírez, all he could obtain was an interview with technical specialists, but given the topic, they requested a written explanation regarding why he mentioned North America and Russia. On April 8, 1952, he sent his reply:

> The discovery that I made in these *discos* [saucers] is the result of my work as a naturalist. I want to charge around $100,000 for my work. The bundle of information will be made available to the Merchant Marine and to military vessels that will be the most likely to encounter them and would be stunned emotionally if they encountered these mysterious flying saucers.[54]

For that reason he insisted once again that the president meet with him. At that point the paper trail ended, and Sr. Robles did not succeed in meeting the president. Arturo Navarrete from San Juan province met the same fate. He wanted to get together with the president to express his gratitude to Argentina, where he had resided after coming from Spain forty years earlier. He also spoke vaguely of ideas that would enable Argentina to make millions. This meeting never took place.[55]

The widow of a trusting man found out that an invention could be widely advertised without any recompense to the inventor or the family. Impoverished, he wrote directly to the president in October 1953 complaining that her husband's letter had never received any response since he sent it, along with his suggestions, in March 1952. She seemed to be blaming the president for her predicament. What the woman really sought was a pension for herself in her old age. She received nothing.[56]

Other imaginative ideas came to the Ministry of Technical Affairs. One involved a cure for cancer derived from the roots of plants. The author presented photos, presumably before and after the treatment that lasted thirty-five days. This man wanted to meet with the president. However, the ministry wanted more details that never appeared.[57]

Children and the Second Five-Year Plan

After Perón was reelected in 1952, the government disseminated a pamphlet that provided a way for teachers to discuss economic and social development

with children. It began with a quote by Perón: "Every Argentine has the duty
to watch out and make sure that the plan is fulfilled. Sabotage betrays the
Patria; sloth is culpable neglect and will be punished by the State." Following
this severe statement came a letter telling children that the way they could
defend the nation was "to know, disseminate, and fulfill the second five-year
plan."[58] Subsequent pages presented the basic ideas of both five-year plans as
efforts to promote patriotism and national greatness.

This pamphlet compared Perón's two plans to the battle plans formed by
the Argentine hero of independence, José de San Martín. It advised children
to pray that they had fulfilled their obligations to the plan. "You are a soldier
in this battle. . . . I know that you will defend with all your heart the two flags
of Peronism: the happiness of the people and the greatness of the nation."[59]

Evidently all public-school children in the fifth and sixth grades from 1953
to 1955 had to read the pamphlet. That reality, along with children's ability to
write to Juan and Eva through the magazine *Mundo Peronista* (1951–1955),
ensured that a generation of children had the opportunity to experience
charismatic bonds with their leaders.

In retrospect, we can see that the Segundo Plan Quinquenal was doomed
to failure, as the president was overthrown in 1955 and the government faced
increased restiveness and high inflation. Regardless of the reality, however,
the plan succeeded in its effort to reach out to disenfranchised Argentines
throughout the country, including those who previously might have counted
on Eva. Although few of them were rewarded with personal interviews with
the president, many received responses from the Ministry of Technical
Affairs and learned that some of their ideas were already scheduled for
implementation in the Segundo Plan Quinquenal. This communication, as
well as those failed efforts to promote inventions and demand succor for
specific individuals, had far-reaching effects on the electorate—even after
Eva's death and the decline of Juan's popularity among urban workers and
other interest groups that demanded even more benefits than they had here-
tofore received. In contrast, inhabitants of the countryside still hoped for a
reversal of bad situations that confronted them.

CHAPTER 5

Children and *la Patria*

FOR A SIGNIFICANT number of letter writers who were parents in the 1940s and 1950s, the future of their children was paramount. They wrote to dedicate their children to the nation, or la patria, because they did not have the means to provide for their needs. These letters came to replace those that had earlier been directed to institutions of charity such as the Society of Beneficence and state-run institutions that dealt with delinquent children. Argentines had also appealed to the thousands of smaller entities operated by immigrant and religious communities, but by the 1940s these waned in importance as Peronism began to implement social justice and the welfare state and as internal migrants replaced immigrants as the community most in need in Buenos Aires. Logic would suggest that letter writing should have become less important as the welfare state expanded. Nevertheless, an ethos based in the allure of personal communication between the people and their leaders—one that had historical roots and also the explicit endorsement of the Peróns—continued to animate a large sector of the population.

One important theme with a long history continued to appear in letters: the desire of parents that the state mold their children into worthy citizens. The letters that referred to la patria perceived that it was the social responsibility of parents and the state to make sure that children grew up well educated and healthy enough to serve the nation as workers, soldiers, or—in the case of girls—future mothers. Native-born Argentines and immigrants whose children were born in Argentina alike held this relatively uncomplicated view of the nation-state.

Before we can explore this group of letters written to Juan and Eva, we should look at some historical precedents. In the late nineteenth and early twentieth century—before the rise of obligatory military service after 1901 (abolished in 1994)—abandoned, delinquent, and orphaned boys most commonly became dedicated to la patria by their parents, who sent them to reform schools, or through the practice of transferring them from state orphanages to serve in the military. Such boys, regardless of whether they lived in the Society of Beneficence's Boys' Orphanage or were fostered out by public defenders of children (men authorized to handle the problems of abandoned children or orphans) or the Society of Beneficence, all faced the reality that without fathers, the military would train them. Indeed, the damas of the society viewed their charges as ideal military recruits. Lacking fathers, officials reasoned that the boys belonged to the fatherland.

This policy began as early as 1874, when Sra. Jacinta Castro, an employee at the Boys' Orphanage, created the Maipú Battalion to train the boys in military maneuvers. Their instructor, a man who had been cashiered for taking part in a political rebellion, himself became rehabilitated as he taught boys discipline and instilled military principles. The girls sewed the boys' uniforms as well as their own, and after six years the boys received their first rifles.[1] The Boys' Orphanage became so committed to military education that the damas criticized public schools for excluding it and accused them of "feminizing" boys instead of teaching them to defend the nation. If other young men learned how to work to defend the nation, then they, too, would be ideal candidates for military service.[2] Well before military service was made obligatory, this idea became popular at other boys' orphanages and their inmates were also funneled into military service as soon as they reached legal age.

But even younger boys could be sent to the military, primarily to serve as musicians. Their lack of discipline and education usually led military officials to return these immature recruits to the orphanages. Orphan males ended up in the military both before and after 1901. The Cabin-Boys' School (Escuela de Grumetes) took some of these minor children in the 1890s to serve in the military band, but by 1911 the school no longer accepted minors. Other schools also raised the admission age to nineteen, the age at which time all cadets became subject to the military code. Subsequently, most boys left orphanages at the age when they could fulfill this requirement.[3]

The Society of Beneficence also offered up orphan girls to serve la patria by sewing, as it sought contracts for work from government or commercial entities. On a number of occasions the damas sought contracts with the military to provide employment for the girls and to defray the costs of their education. In the case of the military these deals usually involved sewing uniforms and other garments. To make the contracts both competitive and enticing, on at least one occasion the society tried to undercut competition from factories by offering the services of orphans at no salary. Despite the desire to obtain low bids, not even the military could accept such conditions.[4]

Another agency that aided children, the Child Protection Society (Patronato de la Infancia) founded by the municipality of Buenos Aires after the financial crash of 1890 and operated by elite men, set up its first school for vagrant boys in October 1894 after reading that the police had rounded up homeless youth and placed them in correctional institutions instead of homes run by charities. The Patronato not only wanted to provide humane conditions for them but, like the Society of Beneficence, wanted to educate them in vocational arts and make them "useful and honest citizens for society." The first school was open only to children born in Argentina who had been abandoned or maltreated or whose parents were too poor or too incapacitated to educate them. Eventually the Patronato allowed admission to immigrant children who had resided in Argentina for three years.[5]

Francisco P. Moreno, a naturalist, explorer, and politician, founded the first national park in Argentina as well as the Patriotic Schools (Escuelas Patrias) on his own property to rescue boys from picking through trash dumps for food. The Patronato de la Infancia soon took over his efforts in March 1907, and by 1909 eight hundred boys attended. At the school, the boys learned Argentine history and how to celebrate patriotic festivals, chant the national anthem, and say the catechism, along with basic subjects.[6]

A 1914 report issued by the Patronato explained that even before teaching boys about patriotism, teachers had to work incessantly to keep them from bringing firearms into the classroom. "Those poor boys had no notion of family or patria. . . . It was difficult to establish discipline by affection and by respect." One member of the patronato's Governing Council (Comisión Directiva) had noted that "children were used to being beaten by some of the teachers and that teachers had to be trained how to use more subtle methods to obtain order and attention."[7]

Other efforts of the Patronato included the founding of a school dedicated to educating impoverished girls to love la patria. Aided by significant donations from wealthy patrons, eventually several baby-care centers were also established. The number of schools grew in the early twentieth century and provided hot meals and civic education for poor boys and girls.[8] In the 1930s these efforts were emulated by boarding schools constructed in the provinces for the indigenous as well as other poor children.

Despite the efforts of the Society of Beneficence and the Patronato de la Infancia, in the nineteenth century, most abandoned and street children still ended up imprisoned rather than in the military. There were simply too many for the municipal defenders of minors to place in private homes, and fewer boys than girls ended up as domestic servants.[9] Street children, mostly boys, also found their way to reformatories along with orphans. The Correctional Home for Minor Boys of the National Capital that opened in 1899 housed boys indicted and sentenced, those sent by defenders of minors, and youngsters remanded directly by the police, all of whom were supposed to be between the ages of eight and eighteen. The task of the asylum was to shape them into "virtuous men and good citizens."[10]

Clearly the passage of mandatory military service for all Argentine male citizens in 1901 did not solve the problems of boys under the age of eighteen. Nor could the penal institutions described above accommodate all the requests for incarceration. Just as the state directed abandoned children and juvenile offenders to serve la patria, fathers also wanted their boys to serve the nation, particularly if the children did not obey them. In 1909 Ramón Domínguez wrote to the minister of justice complaining of the poor behavior of his seventeen-year-old son. Domínguez placed part of the blame on his wife's more tolerant attitude, but he worried that the juvenile was a bad influence on his other children. "With the certainty that in such a pernicious environment my son will only become a dangerous individual and even less useful to the Nation, to Society, and to the Home," Domínguez pleaded that his son Alberto be sent to the Marcos Paz facility to turn him into a "dignified citizen, honorable, laborious, and as patriotic as the fervent desire of my father's heart."[11]

Mothers had similar fears. On April 9, 1910, Ramona Paloma sent a letter to the minister of justice insisting that the state allow her son Raimundo to enter reform school. As she put it, "I cannot control him and my efforts as a mother have been completely useless to make him observe good conduct and his bad inclinations lead me to do this." She added that her husband had disappeared fifteen years earlier and the boy was "on the road to perdition." She concluded with the statement *"Es lei"* (It's the law) in reference to the civil code.[12]

By the mid-1940s and the election of Juan Perón to the presidency, many things had changed in Argentina, but persistent poverty (often ignored in the tales of the rich pampas), the ever-increasing migration of families from the interior to Buenos Aires, and the continued disintegration of families all compelled parents to write letters with the hope that their children might serve la patria through the intervention of Juan and Eva. In July 1947, for example, *El Laborista* reported that the government was very concerned about the number of homeless people *sin techo* (without a roof over their heads) and authorized the rehabilitation of a building to house nine families with twenty minors and two unmarried women who were living under a bridge in the Palermo neighborhood. It was precisely the situations of these families that, in fact, led to the first hogar de tránsito founded by Eva.[13]

Among the early letters to Eva, Graciela de Franco wrote to the intervener Dr. Méndez San Martín, urging him to contact Eva:

Very respectfully, I have been unable to speak with *our beloved Lady of Hope* (because I have gone five times to the welfare and labor offices without gaining an audience with her). . . . As an Argentine and *a Patriot* Dr. I ask you with great tenderness to see that this this letter reaches the hands of this marvelous Eva so that she can determine if this case is deserving of the great work of charity she performs daily.

My concern is about five tiny children whom Eva loves so dearly. . . . A month ago a twenty-nine-year-old lady died leaving six little ones in the greatest despair, almost naked, without shoes, and all thin. The father is desperate because he works and has to leave them alone. In the name of God and la Patria I ask the Doctor to intercede before our dear Evita. . . . signed Graciela de Franco.[14]

One child went to the Instituto Mercedes de Lasala y Riglos on November 29, 1947. That, however, was not enough and Graciela wrote once again to tell Dr. Méndez San Martín what a shame it was that naked children still roamed the streets.

We have no more information on these poor children, but most likely they were placed in orphanages. Since files were organized by both name and date of entry of a child into the system, it makes tracking families difficult unless the file numbers of siblings appear in other files. The importance of this letter is that it uses the term Lady of Hope very early on, and it is one of the very few that addressed Eva as Evita.

In contrast to the familiarity with which Graciela wrote, a widower who lived in General Pacheco, Buenos Aires province, sent a more formal letter to "la Señora Doña María Eva Duarte de Perón" on November 20, 1947. After first asking the First Lady to pardon him for bothering her, he went on to explain his painful situation. He addressed her "as the only life raft to save him from his suffering." His thirteen-year-old son, Omar, had become "disobedient" and was headed for trouble. As a traveling fruit vendor without relatives whose wife had died many years ago, the father found it impossible to "exercise his paternal authority" over the boy. He had already sought help from the Office of Minors within the Secretariat of Labor and Welfare with no result. "Disillusioned already, I come to you with the intimate hope that your pious soul and noble heart will give me the satisfaction that I have not achieved after wandering about in search of the salvation of future soldier of the patria who carries my blood."

Eva obtained a quick but not necessarily enthusiastic response from the Patronato Nacional de Menores, the national agency that operated juvenile reformatories, and in January 1948 Omar entered the Ricardo Gutiérrez Home, a reformatory where sentenced boys, street children, and unruly sons all lived together, with only a second-grade education. He remained in there until April 1950.

Petitioners had begun to write to Juan Perón even before his election. One of the earliest letters dates from March 27, 1944. María Alsina sent a letter addressed to the "Secretary of Labor and Welfare, Col. Juan D. Perón." The accompanying file explained that María had worked for several years as a maid in Buenos Aires, while her son lived with relatives in Tucumán province in northwest Argentina. María, like many women who migrated to the capital city in the 1930s and 1940s, had a broken marriage. With little education, the type of jobs she could find offered neither lodging nor tolerance for children. The boy subsequently went to other relatives in Santiago del Estero where he remained until he was eleven, when his mother wrote this letter to Juan in 1944:

As it is public and notorious that the Coronel patriotically aids the sons of this land, I ask you to intercede in the National Child Protection Agency, so that my son can enter the Almafuerte Trade School. . . . I ask you to do this for us because that way he will be near me. I wouldn't be able to visit him if he were interned in a school outside the Capital.

I ask you once again to forgive me for disturbing you and the tasks you have proposed for the good of the nation, and for all we true criollos hope and want.[15]

This letter is important not only for its early date, but also because the petitioner saw a bond with Juan through children, something that would be reiterated time and again. Furthermore, María signed her letter as a criolla to prove her *argentinidad*. She also clearly indicated elsewhere in the letter that she was not a single mother. Finally, she insisted that she wanted the child to go to school close to where she worked and lived, thereby proving her own credentials as a mother.

Two months later, on May 5, 1944, Perón's secretariat contacted the Almafuerte school and the president of the Patronato Nacional de Menores, noted criminologist Carlos de Arenaza, who answered him on May 12.[16] Arenaza informed Perón that José would have to attend Los Arenales School in Ingeniero Maschwitz, Buenos Aires province, because the boy was too young to enroll in the Almafuerte school. However, once the boy arrived at Los Arenales, doctors determined that he suffered from a condition, subsequently identified as epilepsy, and he was then sent to the Almafuerte school, which in turn wanted to transfer him to the Children's Hospital. However, both good medical treatment and the presence of his mother enabled him to remain at the Almafuerte school until July 1950, when his mother took custody of the boy.

While this case was complicated by José's seizures, the bureaucratic effort necessary for Perón's office to answer María distracted Perón from other issues under scrutiny, first of the secretariat and then of the presidency. These early experiences most likely revealed to Juan that, while all efforts to build a welfare state were important, there would always be the need for a personal touch. And his wife provided that personal connectivity.

Equally important, the story of María and José proved to be the first of many exchanges of correspondence between ordinary people and the Peróns.

Many petitioners cared little for the niceties of bureaucratic realities and government plans. Their concerns about their children, their old age, their infirmities, and their poverty—not programs—motivated their correspondence.

President Perón, of course, was treated with similar respect and often called General, Presidente, or both. He received a letter from a woman late in December 1947 about her nephews, who lived in a rural part of the Chaco. In it the aunt uses language similar to words employed by President Sarmiento in the early nineteenth century to describe the barbarism of the Argentine countryside at that time. She refers to herself in the third person until she makes her request. At that time she identifies herself as the author of the letter.

> I, Regina B. Kabbi, . . . have taken charge of the education of my nephews Carlos and Natán Kabbi, eleven and nine years old respectively. This was done to safeguard the mental and physical health of the boys who were living in an inhospitable area of the Chaco (Quitilipo) with their parents and four younger brothers. The struggle for survival in this rude and uncivilized area absorbed the attention of their parents, and for this reason I decided to rescue them from this semi-barbarianism in which they lived to also relieve my brother and father-in-law of this task. The boys learned to read and write in primary school . . . but now . . . I feel discouraged that I will never turn these children into useful citizens. Bad habits learned from an untamed childhood have affected these children and their guardians are unable to provide them the right direction, especially when her job that supports them prevents her from watching them constantly. But they can still be useful citizens.
>
> How hopeful I am that government aid will help me to mold the wayward and primitive nature of these boys by identifying for me some school, institute or other establishment to which they can be sent!
>
> It will be the salvation for the nation that they should be and without a doubt can be dignified sons of our strong and generous nation.[17]

The aunt clearly wanted to take custody of the children from their relatives in the Chaco. The bureaucratic response noted that the aunt removed the children from the Chaco because of the perceived inappropriate influence they received from the local indigenous people and because they were far from school. Once she obtained her wishes and the children moved to Buenos Aires, the situation was still not ideal as the aunt worked at the elegant Gath y Chaves department store on Florida Street in downtown Buenos Aires, but the boys lived at the Ricardo Gutiérrez Home because their aunt did not earn enough to support them. Later, another brother joined them, and they remained at the home until 1954. In this case an aunt successfully pleaded with Juan Perón to send her nephews to a reform school. While it might seem inappropriate for someone not from the immediate family to turn one's own relatives over to juvenile authorities, in early twentieth-century Argentina fears of juvenile independence and behavior were sufficient to threaten all structures of authority.

Letters from parents and other family members continued to flow into the offices of both Peróns. One way we know this is that copies of the letters remained in the archives of the Consejo Nacional de Niños. This archive, in turn, became housed with the Society of Beneficence papers in the Consejo's archives. They were not threatened by the burning of documents at the Eva Perón Foundation and elsewhere. Because of this we learn that Eva received a letter on January 3, 1948, from a widowed Spanish resident who addressed Eva as the Lady of Hope.

As a Spanish woman, I live in a country where you have served as an ambassador of peace, and (after your trip to Spain) you brought back so many grateful memories, memories that make the mothers of that land so proud. We Spanish women have come to this great nation in order to make it even greater by giving it Argentine children. Please permit me to write to you with the knowledge that you, the friend of all souls, whatever their cause, will help. As a mother I ask you to intercede before the authorities of the Patronato de Menores so that my eleven-year-old son, named Rómulo Masón can be helped. I have lost my husband and am left with four sons. Rómulo is the youngest, and against my wishes and those of his brothers, he does not want to follow the path of good behavior. When he goes off to school, he joins other boys and plays hooky, to such an extreme that he neither knows how to read nor write, and since it has been several years since I began the paperwork in the named institute without hearing anything, it is for this reason that I bother you as I know that it will not disappear into space and thus my son can become useful to the patria.[18]

This letter is significant because until the 1940s, Spanish immigrants relied on their own charitable organization, the Patronato Español. After the letter was sent, a report from the Directorate of Minors (Dirección de Menores) showed that experts disagreed about Rómulo. Some believed that he had mental disabilities, while others opined that his learning disability was behavioral. After spending time in several institutions, he was sent to the Ricardo Gutiérrez Home, and his mother was charged five pesos per month, most likely because, unlike the child, she was not a citizen. The mother evidently changed her mind and did not leave her son in the home for very long, and by December 18 he returned to his family. Once again a mother's wishes, as well as her nationality, trumped the state's ability to reform children.

The Peróns also listened to fathers. On February 9, 1948, Ronaldo Quilmes wrote,

> Please forgive me, Your Excellency, but I believe in your elevated sense of humanity and I hope to be one of those most favored by your works. I am the father of seven sons. One of my fourteen children disgracefully has entered a world of perverse instincts and despite the fact that I have dedicated all my energy to direct him on the good path, I have not succeeded. It is only with great effort that I compelled him to finish the fourth grade, but his bad inclinations still induce him to be disrespectful and disobedient. Today, lured by his love of the streets, he has taken the decision to flee from home, an act that will inevitably lead him to become a vagabond and perhaps a delinquent.
>
> My desire as a father is that this boy becomes a dignified man, useful for the patria. For this reason I ask your excellency to help me place him in some boarding school where the child will receive education and discipline.[19]

In January 1949 the boy also entered the Ricardo Gutiérrez Home.

Even when parents wrote to other officials, just dropping the president's name could elicit help and redeem a child for la patria. On April 10, 1948, Florencia de Guillermo wrote to the Directorate of Minors, asking to place her twelve- and thirteen-year-old sons in the Ricardo Gutiérrez Home. Florencia had six children and an almost completely blind husband. In her request she recalled the words of Perón, stating, "And I also want to give my country useful men. To achieve that they must have the culture and education that cannot be found here in Patagonia where there are neither adequate schools nor work for myself or for them."[20] The issue of poor-quality education and/or the lack of schools became a central issue of parents in the 1940s and 1950s. In the ensuing investigation, the children were deemed fit to attend school and the situation of the family deemed precarious due to the husband's disability. Although we have no paperwork regarding what happened subsequently, it is most likely that the children went off to Buenos Aires to attend school.

That May, Eva received another letter asking for help for a child. As we can see from the following letter, this was not the first time Eva had helped Armando F.

I pray to God that this message will reach you as you will share the suffering of an Argentine citizen who needs your help so desperately. My wife died in a hospital in General Rodríguez of pulmonary TB, leaving me with a four-year old son and I don't have anyone to care for him. I pray to you Sra., as the great humanitarian, that you take pity on a father whose little son needs help and place him in a school where he will be cared for like so many others.

I am handicapped by the loss of a leg, and thanks to you I have obtained an artificial leg so that I can now walk better and work honestly to earn a little for my survival and that of my son whom I madly adore.[21]

When Eva did not answer immediately, Armando sent another letter in November 1950, this time emphasizing his concerns about la patria:

I beg you bountiful Sra. de Perón to help place my son in some boys' school where tomorrow he will become a dignified citizen and a man useful to our great Patria. Into your generous hands, I hand the future of my dear little son Paco.

With all my heart I thank you for fulfilling this favor I ask, and I ask God to bestow on you, gentle Sra., and your dignified husband, eternal health, happiness, and the eternal love from the people who adore you, as loyally, as humble descamisados. Thanks to you and the great Illustrious leader, this little boy might learn and have a piece of bread.[22]

Armando's comment on a piece of bread brought out the specific intent that he and other poor rural parents had—placement of their children in a boarding school where they would be lodged and fed, not just educated. As with many of these requests, Armando specified where he would like the boy to be sent, so that Armando could visit Paco with ease. However, these requests could not always be granted, as the state tended to move the children around according to their age and their behavior.

In December 1950 little Paco was admitted to the Instituto Mercedes de Lasala y Riglos by order of the Dirección General de Asistencia Social. When he turned seven, he went to the General José de San Martín boys' home. His grandmother was able to care for him between 1952 and 1954. Then he was sent to the General Martín Rodríguez home. Paco did not flourish in this environment. He refused to study and keep things in order. The following year he was sent to the Almafuerte school to complete his studies and then he finally returned to his father. The child's report showed how the circulation of children among family members, a long-standing tradition in Argentina, continued to provide additional support for parents. It also conveyed the complex reactions of children to being shuttled around both institutions and family members. In this sense, Paco's experience typified the emotional turmoil of children living in unstable situations.[23]

Bonita de Martínez, who lived in the Buenos Aires working-class suburb of Avellaneda, wrote Eva in 1948 asking for help. Her husband had abandoned her and her two children in Corrientes province. Forced to go to Buenos Aires to work, she left one child with a brother and brought her ten-year-old child with her. The latter boy could neither read nor write, and she had difficulty enrolling him in school. She wished that he could "become a good soldier, defender of his Patria," but she couldn't afford to put him in a boarding school. Because she worked as a domestic servant and lived in, she couldn't keep the boy with her.[24]

In 1949 the boy entered the Hogar General Martín Rodríguez in the province of Buenos Aires. Two years later, through the Peronist Party, the mother asked that he be transferred to the school in which she then worked as a domestic. Evidently that, too, failed to work out, as the file contains several letters written by the mother to her son, Conrado.

Many of those who wrote to Juan and Eva about entrusting children to the Patria were plagued by illness in the family. In Marta Lupini's first letter to Eva on September 14, 1948, she pleaded with the First Lady for an opportunity to speak to her about her four children. Separated from her insane husband and living with her elderly parents, Marta begged Eva for help, noted that she was a fervent Peronist, and sent her regards to President General Perón. When she did not hear anything, on January 3, 1949, Marta told Eva she had written to the Society of Beneficence, but had received no response. Calling Eva "our *hada buena*" (our good fairy), she again asked that her two sons be placed in school so that "tomorrow they will be dignified men of la Patria who have as a leader a man whose name is synonymous with nobility and giving, General Perón."[25]

By February 1949 an official inspector had turned up at Marta's house. He determined that Marta earned a meager living washing clothes and could not take a better job. Despite this desperate situation, the welfare-state bureaucracy worked too slowly for Marta and in April she again wrote to the First Lady. Finally, after it was determined that the four children were illiterate because they had no schooling and that their father was indeed insane as a consequence of alcoholism, the children—first the older brother Nicolás and then the other three—went to Los Arenales School. The children remained until 1956 when Marta retrieved them. These letters show that as the welfare state evolved, Eva became its public face, and people often became frustrated that she could not produce instant miracles for them.

National holidays could serve as the backdrop to emphasize the relationship between the writers and la patria. One woman from the town of Can-Can, in the territory of Comodoro Rivadavia, wrote to Eva Perón on July 9, 1949—Independence Day—seeking succor:

I am a thirty-six-year-old single woman, born in Can-Can. I write to request help securing lodging for my three little minor children and myself. I am currently in this Capital [Comodoro Rivadavia], but I need to go to Buenos Aires and the city of Córdoba.

My daughters and I are ill. The municipality of this locality secured free passages to Buenos Aires for me and my children so I then can go on to Córdoba to try to save myself and my little daughters. The Municipal Hospital doctor here has advised me to do this. . . . I am completely poor, and I am trying to work part-time to survive, but in reality each day I work. I suffer from a pulmonary infection and my youngest son, five years old, for several months has been in the hospital here, but the doctors all say . . . that it is the climate that makes us suffer the most.

Thank God I have encountered people who have taken pity on me. Upon seeing my bad situation, they have given me work so that I don't die of hunger. I also know that the illness that affects myself and my children is not the easiest to cure.

For this reason, Sra., I write to you with the knowledge of all the good that you do for the poor. . . . We have no resources and bad luck follows us. I know Sra. that this letter has reached you and I am sure that my plea will not be useless, and I plead for temporary lodgings for us until we can save ourselves. I have three children, two boys and Anita. I don't know where the father is and, forgive me, but it is not necessary to know, because you are the only person who can save all of us.

I am very poor, but I want to save the children. Perhaps tomorrow they can be useful and give back to the Patria some of what it gives to them. Equally important, they are innocents and know nothing of evil or good and I only ask for them.

Distinguished Sra., I leave as soon as I am granted the passages in the Administration of the YPF [the state petroleum monopoly]. I don't want to land in the national Capital not knowing where to go and be completely desperate. I know absolutely no one in Buenos Aires and no one can protect me and I don't want to arrive there only to suffer more.

I beg of you to take all this into consideration and answer me as soon as possible so that it will be possible to count on your protection for our security.[26]

Eva sent the letter on to the Society of Beneficence, which was under federal intervention at that time, and on July 27 they responded that the mother and the three children could stay at the Dispensario Central María Ferrer, originally a dependency of the Society of Beneficence. Then in September the two youngest entered homes run by the society while the older boy was admitted to a hospital. The mother got a job as a maid at a hotel and was allowed to stay there, and furthermore she was able to visit all three children. Thus, through the efforts of Eva Perón and the Society of Beneficence, the entire family received help and remained as intact as possible.

Another letter written in 1949 to Eva at once expounded José Provano's needs and the desire to make the Patria proud of his children. In this case he wanted to meet personally with the wife of the president.

> It is a great honor to write to you as I respectfully ask to have a meeting with you as soon as possible regarding the following: I am the father of six children, and my wife is hospitalized in this city.
>
> I have lived in Buenos Aires for two years, during which time it has been completely impossible to have my children by my side because I can't find housing that will permit me to go and get my children who live now in San Gregorio, Santa Fe.
>
> In view of this grave situation I find myself in I have to pay someone to care for my children and my salary is insufficient to cover expenses. I ask Your Excellency to take the necessary measures to solve my anguishing problem by placing my children in State establishments so that they can have the education necessary to become future citizens, of which the patria can be proud.
>
> I anxiously await the honor of an audience so that I can express myself personally in a satisfactory way.[27]

In addition to José's letter, his wife also wrote from her sickbed to urge the First Lady to help them out. Since the mother had been hospitalized, the children had remained with their grandparents but received no financial help from their parents. Although there is no indication that José met Eva, their daughter Bárbara was interned in the Crescencia Boado de Garrigós home, where she remained until 1952 when she returned to the family home in Santa Fe.

Even children recognized their value to la patria. On July 21, 1950, Eduardo Gil wrote to Eva asking for admission to a boarding school. He had already filled out paperwork with the Defender of Minors. His story was a sad one.

> I am ten years old and the woman who has raised me since I was young

can't keep me anymore. My story is very sad. My two sisters live in the
city of La Plata because my parents are ill. For this reason I ask you very
tenderly to grant me this wish, because I want to be a man who is useful
to la Patria and who can learn from the teachings that General Perón
gives us.[28]

Evidently Eduardo did not get into the boarding school he wanted. He was
sent out to the Marcos Paz reformatory, very far from his grandmother, who
was too old to travel that far. Completely determined, he sent another letter
to Eva reiterating his situation and claiming that he had no money for school
or for clothes. He also implored her in the

> name of General Perón (who affirms that in the Argentine Republic
> the only privileged ones are the children). I love him although I have
> never spoken to him and I implore you, my lady, the mother of the
> helpless, to help. Each time I hear you on the radio I am sad that I am not
> close enough to you to hug you for the things you do in such a selfless
> fashion.[29]

This time Eduardo was sent to the General San Martín boys' home; he
remained in state-subsidized reform schools until he reached the age of
twenty-one.

Juan Gormendi also wrote several desperate letters to Eva, whom he identified as "La Digníssima 'Dama de la Esperanza'" (The Most Dignified Lady
of Hope) from January 23, 1950, until June of that year. A lowly railroad
worker, he did not dare to call her Evita. A widower, he had three little children who lived with their grandparents in Las Breñas in the Chaco. From his
meager salary, he managed to send his parents 150 pesos per month, but that
was only enough to make them "people who could survive the struggle for
life." For that reason, he hoped that Eva could find the children a place in an
educational institution and serve as a surrogate mother for them.[30]

After having his situation confirmed by the authorities in the province of
Buenos Aires, Juan wrote again on March 6, this time expressing his desire
that his children not only be prepared for the struggle for life, but also
become "useful for society."[31] Then on June 4 he sent another letter. When he
received no response, Eduardo then wrote to the president of the Railroad

Workers' Union and asked him to intervene in favor of his children. Finally the eldest boy, aged seven, was admitted to the General Martín Rodríguez home, where he remained until 1953.

In July 1950 a man wrote Eva Perón from the province of Buenos Aires, asking to find an appropriate institution for his handicapped son. The twelve-year-old child, a victim of infantile paralysis since the age of four, had learned to walk with a cane. Given that the father had six other children, they had no money to send the child to school. He wanted his son to learn a trade that would enable him to find work but also benefit the Patria—"un oficio para bien de él y de la patria." By 1951 the boy had been admitted to a school where officials discovered that he needed far more therapy than they could provide there. The government sent the boy to a hospital where he underwent a successful course of treatment.[32]

That same month Eva received a letter concerning a child who had been mistreated by his father and sent to live with a woman who treated him better. His mother, a victim of tuberculosis, had to abandon him at birth to keep him healthy. A woman who worked at the Preventorio Rocca, an asylum to help TB-prone children, took care of him after the age of six. Given his father's abusive behavior, eventually the boy's uncle was named his guardian. When he was ten, the son, Eduardo himself, petitioned Eva Perón to keep his father from making him return to the family. Eduardo asked instead to be placed in a school run by her "because your great compassion for children is my only security." He went on to say that the woman who had cared for him for so many years could no longer do so. To reaffirm the importance of Eva's help, he insisted, "I want to be a good man who will be useful to the patria and learn the lessons taught by General Perón."

Social workers mentioned that Eduardo had run away from his parents' home because of bad treatment. They also described the home as a place "without culture where material, moral, and physical misery prevailed." They reaffirmed that placing him in school was the only way that he could become a "man useful for society."[33] Evidently the September 1950 report did not prevail and the boy remained with his family. Thus on January 16, 1951, Eduardo again wrote to Eva.

> I have always been a fervent admirer of the social work of your foundation. It enables many who have been bereft of good luck to reap

your generosity. I fervently desire that you examine my situation. I have told you what a fair solution would be so once again I dare to divert your attention in order to place my case in your hands. . . . Approximately two months ago my grandmother filled in the necessary paperwork . . . to find a vacancy in a school as I do not have the means to pay for my studies and buy clothes. Four months after I wrote to you I was assigned a place in school far away in Marcos Paz, Buenos Aires. As my grandmother is elderly, I could not accept the vacancy because she could not travel and I don't want to be far from her.

Evidently Eduardo tried to get an appointment to see Eva but was told by the Women's Peronist Committee with whom he consulted that such a meeting would be very difficult. As a result Eduardo was living with his grandmother, sleeping in the kitchen as there was no other place for him.[34]

He concluded his note invoking General Perón, "who affirms that in Argentina the only privileged ones are the children," and Eva, "the mother of the underprivileged." He claimed to listen to both of them on the radio and only hoped to be able to embrace them one day. As he was sure that his wishes would be fulfilled, he reiterated his hope "that in the future I will be a citizen useful to the Great Argentina." By May he had his wish come true and was placed in the General San Martín home.

The story, however, did not have a happy ending. As in the earlier case of Paco, the hardships he faced for several years came to affect his behavior. At school he began to demonstrate rage and threw temper tantrums. Nevertheless, he remained in the care of institutions until he reached the age of majority in 1966.[35]

Executive Pardons for Children

The last set of letters I have found that relate directly to concepts of la patria deal with pardons for minors who committed crimes. In celebration of the anniversary of the death of General José de San Martín, President Perón issued Decree 17.252 on August 16, 1950, stipulating the requisites for pardons and which types of crimes could be excluded. Perón reduced sentences to thirty days' incarceration, effectively eliminating all those inmates whose crimes were covered by the national criminal code. The only inmates ineligible for pardons consisted of those imprisoned for "crimes against honesty," national security, and violations of Law 11.309 regarding drugs. Crimes against honesty were honor crimes including adultery, rape, murder, and the corruption of minors.[36] I have found several cases of minors who were pardoned by Perón. However, few actually obtained their freedom, because their crimes were by law exempted from pardon or because reformatories or prison officials resisted releasing these prisoners before they served their time.

Parents usually sent the petitions that argued that the children had demonstrated their complete rehabilitation through incarceration. These minors, along with many adults, thus were now worthy of being proclaimed citizens with all the civic rights associated with them. Some parents had asked the president for a pardon even before the San Martín event. Omar Gutiérrez was nineteen when his mother wrote to the Directorate of Minors in 1950 to ask for a pardon. Omar had been imprisoned for robbery and attempted robbery since 1948, at which time she wrote to the president directly. Now she tried to make the case that Omar had been very young when he had committed the crime and that he had fallen in with a bad crowd. This time the letter was forwarded to the minister of justice, Belisario Cache Pirán from the Directorate of Minors, with a report stating that Omar had distinguished himself in his studies and received various prizes for his efforts. For those reasons the directorate asked the president to grant the pardon, deeming it to be "indispensable for stimulating his recuperation, and returning to society a useful citizen."[37] In this case Omar received his pardon at the same time as another minor, Ricardo Coniglione, who had been charged with murder and robbery. Coniglione should never have been pardoned, as he was convicted of the honor crime of murder. Efforts to pardon large numbers of persons often led to inappropriate use the of the pardon law. Perón often pardoned children without paying much attention to the terms of the pardons, and this led to conflicts between prison authorities and the president.

An example of a child who received a presidential pardon as part of the festivities of 1950 is the story of Andrés Ferrero. In 1949 he was convicted of complicity in the crime of murder, but from the very beginning neighbors had suggested that he was innocent. After judicial officials interviewed his mother as well as his neighbors, President Perón, without a personal letter from anyone, reduced Andrés's sentence to thirty days. However, the

Directorate of Minors refused to carry out the pardon, as the boy did not
fulfill all the requirements of the decree since he had been accused of com-
mitting a "crime against honesty." Indeed, it turns out he was one of six
boys turned down by the director of minors, Pedro R. Bagnatti, for not
fulfilling the mandates of the law.[38] Either the president or his counselors
did not read the files closely or they wanted the president to exceed his
authority, something the director of minors refused to allow. It remains to
be investigated whether this happened to adults as well. It also appears that
officials granted arbitrary pardons just like the president. One might argue
that the release of pardoned prisoners became a terrain of conflict between
judicial authorities and the executive office, and the politics of charisma
proved to be the cause.

 Parents may have wanted to send their recalcitrant boys to jail, but they
did not believe that la patria had any right to convict their innocent children.
This meant that la patria was supposed to correct any mistakes in the system
of rehabilitating minors. In any case, la patria had its hands full with the
children Eva and Juan sent into its care.

Furthermore, these letters show a clear continuity of expectations on the
part of the Argentine people, who began in the early twentieth century to use
the question of juvenile delinquency and the custody clauses of the Civil
Code to request that the state rehabilitate their children. In order to do this,
from 1899 when the idea of a national reformatory for delinquent boys was
first raised, legislators struggled to enact laws to specifically enable the state
to bypass parental custody under circumstances of parental abandonment or
police arrests so that children could be sent to reform schools. At the same
time, they recognized the ultimate legal rights of parental custody, one that
enabled parents to challenge judicial decisions.

When Juan became president, he and his wife continued to receive petitions from parents who hoped that their children could usefully serve the
country through the intervention of the state. Other parents requested presidential pardons so that their children could be released. Juan and Eva, col-
lectively and as individuals, represented the last hope of many parents for a
dignified future for their children, but that faith was frequently dashed when
prison authorities stuck to the letter of the law.

Whether people wanted material improvements in their lives or help to
prepare the future of their children, the specter of Juan and Eva loomed

large. After Eva died, it eventually became apparent that Juan did not have her instinct for achieving "the greater good" through the performance of charity. Thus, Argentines did not fare as well with Juan, the military man who believed in the capacity of bureaucracy to ensure wellbeing. Furthermore, these stories show how people insisted that the Peronist government, specifically Juan and Eva, should attend to their personal and family problems. Petitioners' success indicated that the bureaucratic welfare state had many hurdles to overcome in Argentina. Petitioning through letter writing posed a formidable obstacle to achieving a bureaucratic welfare state, but Juan and Eva's record for creating children worthy of the Patria and for pardoning children was modest at best.

CHAPTER 6

Charismatic Bonds

How Long Can They Last?

DUAL DISTINCTIVE BUT complementary approaches led to the creation of charismatic bonds through letter writing. The development of Peronist allegiances took far more time than simply implementing the first and second five-year plans. Indeed, it could be argued that the formation of the political machine that led to Juan Perón's election in 1946 marked one of many stages of consolidation. And while the plans provided a political and economic template, maintaining loyalty proved more difficult than even Perón himself might have imagined. Not only did non-Peronist Radical and Socialist legislators vigorously oppose legislation sent to congress by the executive, the president often had to confront opposition from his own political supporters. Furthermore, the Ministry of Technical Affairs did not have sufficient funding to implement all reasonable programs suggested by the citizenry.

This reality became even more evident after Perón's reelection in 1952, at which point the president began to resort more frequently to decrees to implement his programs, and he suddenly found that his charismatic bridge had crumbled. Eva's death on July 26, 1952, added to Perón's difficulties as he subsequently lacked a strong female influence over women—who had obtained the vote in 1947, but who could not participate in national elections until 1952. This chapter focuses once again on those people who either did not have the protection of labor unions or who were too poor to benefit from the increased wages that urban workers enjoyed during his first administration. It reaffirms that women comprised an important component of this group, either as supplicants or as their husbands' defenders.

Dr. Armando Méndez San Martín, on September 25, 1946, forwarded to
the presidential residence two letters received by the Society of Beneficence
but addressed to Eva. On September 18, 1947, Eloisa de Pirelli wrote to the
First Lady with very simple language, complaining of a decision made by the
Society of Beneficence:

> I would like to meet with you Sra. to explain my situation so that I can
> speak with you as a mother. . . . It seems that destiny should have taught
> me, but I had no home and always had to fight for survival and was
> defrauded of my hopes. Sra. I study commercial textile courses in a girls'
> school that the president has put at my disposition and I study with
> enthusiasm so that I can prosper. Once again, I need your help to ensure
> that the National Association of the Blind provides me a job as a matron
> in the dormitories or in the clothing department. I know that there are
> vacancies and to tell you exactly where they are, they are in the San
> Cecilia Home in Villa Linch [sic]. I ask you for a thousand pardons for
> the inconvenience that I cause you as well as my daring, but I know you
> are so bountiful.[1]

The truth of the matter emerged when Dr. Méndez San Martín added his
own note, pointing out that the Society of Beneficence did not control the
National Association for the Blind. Ironically, Juan Perón's own Secretariat
of Labor and Welfare had charge of the agency. The matter seemed to have
been archived and not acted upon, because neither Eva nor Juan had the
bureaucratic facilities to make the association hire the woman. This letter is
just the earliest of many letters written to Eva in care of the Society of Beneficence, her supposedly dreaded enemy, and perhaps for that reason no one
thought to purge the archives of these letters.

While Juan promised many things, followers of Perón and Eva proved
quite willing to exaggerate their leaders' ability to solve personal problems.
Some believed that the Peróns had the absolute political powers attributed to
them by opponents, and loyalists felt no hesitancy to ask them to perform
practical miracles to overcome local political realities. Peronists sought help
not only directly, but also indirectly. They wrote to prominent Peronist officials, including Eva's brother Juan Duarte, Perón's personal secretary during
his first administration; Atilio Renzi, Eva's private secretary; Méndez San

Martín, the intervener of the Society of Beneficence; and Ángel Borlenghi, the socialist labor leader who backed Perón and served as his minister of the interior. Eduardo Elena has already recounted how Raúl Mende, head of the Ministry of Technical Affairs from 1949 to 1955, also became a conduit for petitions, especially from his supporters in the province of Santa Fe. He had particularly close ties to Eva Perón, so he, like Méndez San Martín, smoothed the pathways between the presidential residence and the ministry.[2]

There were other paths to possible Peronist succor. In the archives of the Archivo Intermedio, the national archives devoted to recent history, are several boxes of letters from the Peronist era sent from the Ministry of the Interior. Apparently they had been rescued to prove the crimes of Peronism, and some of the materials formed the documentation for a very anti-Peronist book, *El libro negro de la segunda tiranía* (The Black Book of the Second Tyranny), which referred to the Rosas era as the first tyranny).[3] Most of the documents, however, related to requests for jobs, both from labor unions as well as from individuals. And rather than prove abuse of power, the documents often portray its limits. In many ways, they can be compared to the cache of letters from supplicants for old-age pensions found in the archives of the Society of Beneficence, those that shed light on the role of the Eva Perón Foundation.

Petitions for jobs demonstrate the unwillingness of Peronist supporters to trust an increasingly bureaucratic system—a bureaucracy that was precisely the aim of the two plans. This became very clear when working-class people, particularly those from rural areas, told stories of how the bureaucracies in their local districts left much to be desired, and thus they asked for personal intervention. Even though most of these petitions were accompanied by bureaucratic reports, the *papeleo* (paperwork) meant far less to people forming their charismatic bonds directly to the Peróns.

The Limits of Presidential Influence

Meddling in local politics proved to be difficult for the presidential office. For example, in 1948, after having written several letters about a policeman "who works against our interests," members of an agrarian union wrote to Eva on December 18 asking that the policeman be removed from his position in Pampa del Infierno in the Chaco. Evidently Eva could do nothing, as the district chief of the forest district had already washed his hands of the problem and placed it in the hands of the Ministry of the Interior earlier in November. We do not know how the dispute ended, but clearly locals did not trust authorities in the Chaco who still responded to landowners' interests.[4]

Many people wrote to Juan or Eva seeking back pay. They complained of receiving no salary after being employed to carry out the 1947 national census. As in most countries, census taking in Argentina involves the massive hiring of temporary workers throughout the land. It seems that, in the transition from leaders of the military coup that took place in 1943 until the election of Juan Perón in 1946, many workers did not get paid. One example of distrust of bureaucracy came from Córdoba in 1949 when Leandra de Guiso wrote to Eva Perón about how her husband had never been paid what was owed him for working on the census. Leandra called Eva "the source of justice for the *desamparados* [homeless]" and hoped that the First Lady could help her husband recuperate his daily pay as well as his travel expenses.[5]

Andrés Bianchi, a temporary civil employee in San Juan province, also wrote to Eva. He informed her that he had already sent a complaint to the national tax-accountant agency and had never received an answer.[6] Another man, from Mendoza, was threatened with an embargo on his salary deposited in a bank because he had not been paid over 400 pesos for his services rendered to the census. Either poor bookkeeping or bureaucratic problems seem to have led to delayed payment. After writing to Borlenghi at the Ministry of the Interior and receiving no answer, Salvador Arnot wrote to Eva on July 27, 1949. Salvador claimed he was the son of a widow and that he cared for his minor sister.[7] No additional paperwork accompanied these petitions, and it is highly unlikely that writing to Buenos Aires solved the problems.

Ahmed Akbar, in March 1949, wrote a flowery tribute to Juan and hoped that the president could intercede for him. He identified himself as a fifty-seven-year-old exile, most likely from the collapse of the Ottoman Empire, with forty-one years of residence in

this glorious and hospitable Argentine nation, governed by the dignified and wise illustrious president of the Argentines. I send my wishes for the peace and wellbeing of all on the 9th of July. I also request, confident of your bountiful heart and altruistic feelings, that you intervene in the sad situation in which I suffer.[8]

Ahmed had been imprisoned, according to him, for unjust causes. During that time the police had allowed a sharecropper on his land to live without paying Ahmad and then replaced him with a farmer who had been living there ever since, and whom Ahmed could not dislodge. Furthermore the farmer did not acknowledge Ahmed's ownership claim. Rather than intervene, Perón allowed the ongoing trial to continue until 1950, but the case remained unresolved. Although Ahmed included the entire legal transcript, inquiries revealed that nothing could be done in Río Negro, where the case had taken place.

From the province of Salta, Fernando Leal wrote a flowery and effusive letter to Eva in July 1949. Although addressed to her, the petitioner included Juan in the salutation.

> My dear leaders and father of us all: We poor ones write to request a . . . great favor. I pray that that God and the Virgin of Ledesma will fight the tyrants and traitors of our Patria. . . . I am a sad employee of a police station for the past five years. One day my career ended because of the calumny of a Spaniard who went to our minister of the interior and complained about me. The minister fired me, without verifying the cause because he is a capitalistic guy. Today I am a poor man with . . . three young sons.[9]

Fernando fought the case in court and accused the Spaniard of abusing his authority and leaving him without work for six months. Fernando tried to cover all of his loyalties. His reference to the Virgin of Ledesma demonstrated his strong Catholic faith, and he appealed to Eva as a native-born man, not a foreigner, and certainly as a Peronist and patriot who could tell friends from foes. None of these efforts guaranteed success. Rather than making an outright decision, Eva sent the case to appropriate authorities within the government bureaucracy while the twenty-eight-year-old man waited for help.

One man from Corrientes, Pablo Goyena, wanted an appointment as the head of a civil registry and justice of the peace in Las Breñas, Chaco territory. In September 1949 he wrote to Borlenghi, then minister of the interior, and identified himself as a loyal Peronist. He thought that was sufficient to get a justice of the peace position created by President Perón. Pablo, a retired director of a school, lived in another province and only received a pension of 145 pesos per month, insufficient for his needs. He was willing to take a post anywhere in the Chaco, but he specifically mentioned the one in Las Breñas. Borlenghi evidently looked into the matter and received a note from the Ministry of the Interior of the Chaco territory stating that another man currently occupied the post and that the laws regarding appointments of justice of the peace stated that candidates had to reside in the area. Thus, Pablo did not qualify, and a subsequent letter from the Chaco noted that the petitioner was also too old to qualify for a job with the forestry service. National officials like Borlenghi chose not to fight established laws and local authorities, and since no registry of people who received old-age pensions under the 1946 Peronist decree exists, we cannot tell if Pablo got some additional aid that way.[10]

Aldo Morelli lost his job working for the council to reconstruct the city of San Juan after the terrible earthquake in 1944. Five years later he wrote to Eva complaining that he had been dismissed from his job with the council after working there for two years. He asked her to obtain "through whatever avenues possible, my reincorporation" and he waited "with the absolute security that justice should occur now that we have people who manage the destinies of this Great Argentine Patria who are authentic Argentines." In the last piece of paperwork in this file, local authorities told the General Directorate of the Subsecretariat of the Ministry of the Interior (Dirección General de la Subsecretaría del Ministerio del Interior) of the Chaco that Aldo should not get his job back.[11]

A Peronist supporter of mothers wanted to change the date of Mother's Day. As a representative of the First Argentine Feminine League in Support of Maternity and Children, she wrote to both Eva and Juan on October 21, 1949. The author of this note stated that Mother's Day still had no fixed date in Argentina, and she wanted it changed to October 14. Once this happened, students would learn about motherly love from the first grade onward. Strangely enough, after it was sent to the Ministry of the Interior, it was transferred to the navy, where on February 6, 1950, someone responded that the Catholic Church had staked out March 4 in honor of the festival of Santa Monica, and that the Salvation Army celebrated it on March 8. Furthermore, the Mothers' Club claimed the third Sunday in October, also supported by the Ministry of Education. Thus the navy opined that the Feminine League should not get its wish. On April 1 the Ministry of the Interior formally resolved that October 14 should not be Mother's Day.[12]

Other groups joined in clamoring for aid from Eva. The Social and Sports Club of Floresta wrote to Eva on stationery from an unidad básica (local affiliate) of the Peronist Party and noted that they had seven hundred members asking for help in rehabilitating a building they had acquired. To seal the deal, they claimed to be "united in the sublime trilogy PERÓN-EVITA-MERCANTE" and asked that the "mother of the homeless, first citizen of America" grant their wish. What they wanted was a large piece of land on Remedios Street No. 3748 that belonged to the Ministry of the Interior; the letter was signed by one Pablo d'Agostini. No response was contained in the file, which might signal that no action had been taken but could also mean that the other paperwork had disappeared.[13]

In these "secret" files of the Ministry of the Interior the plight of policemen, as seen in earlier instances, frequently shows up. For example, Juan Correa, who had recently joined the federal police in charge of the city of Buenos Aires, asked for a meeting with Eva in September 1950 to discuss his plight. On September 5 he had been fired, and he wanted to be rehired as a motorman specialist because he had already passed all the exams. Furthermore, he believed he was covered by a presidential decree of January 17, 1947, that protected job security. In this case Eva once again did not act immediately but rather sent the letter to the Ministry of the Interior, where the National Directorate of the National Guard determined that the young man had not been working long enough to fit into the decree. However, since three months had passed since Juan's last employment, he could now try once again to enter the national police. Astoro Bertollo, brigadier general of the federal police, signed the petition on December 14, 1950. In early January they notified Juan. Once again, everything followed bureaucratic procedure, not relying on political intervention.[14]

Other archival sources also recorded failed attempts to appeal for help from Eva and Juan. One poor woman, Amelia, wrote Eva four times beginning in 1949—the last one after the First Lady's death on July 26, 1952—without ever achieving success.

I am sorry to bother you but I need to speak to you about my husband who worked for thirty-two years in a soda factory that he had to leave due to illness and received nothing from them to pay for the necessities of life. I hope that this resonates with your heart and I send my best wishes for your projects as well as those of your husband.[15]

Eva sent the petition to the accident department of the National Directorate of Social Action on February 18, 1949. That same day Amelia wrote Eva another letter stating that her husband had died on December 12, and she found herself alone, ill, and unable to support herself. She followed the letter with one on November 30, 1950, again asking for help and commenting that she had never heard an answer. Only after Eva died and Amelia wrote again did her file arrive at the old-age pension-fund office.

A request from a laundress who lived on a sugar plantation in Tucumán met a similar fate. Although she wrote to Eva in 1950 stating that she was sixty-two years old with young children and provided a certificate of poverty, not until 1953, after Eva died, did the authorities perform an inspection and recommend a pension for her.[16]

Evidence of the limits that constrained the president and First Lady also can be found in the archives of the Society of Beneficence. In March 1951 María Zaída, fifty-three, wrote to Eva from Buenos Aires looking for a job for herself and for her husband, sixty, who had part-time work in a delicatessen and as a waiter due to his advanced age. Marta suffered from asthma and from bronchitis that impeded her desirability as a domestic servant. She begged Eva to find her some work, but a note from September 1951 stated that no work was available for either one, and that a negative response should be sent to them. They did, however, also turn the matter over to the people handling subsidies for the elderly and infirm, and they were approved for an "A" subsidy in 1952 that was not awarded until 1954.[17]

Correspondence from 1951 continued to reveal this inability of Eva to either answer or solve people's problems. Santiago Saone from San Luis del Palma, in the province of Corrientes, wrote to Eva in November. Rather than addressing the letter to the presidential residence, he sent it to the Eva Perón Foundation. Santiago explained that he found himself in a difficult situation: disabled due to a lung infection, married, and with six children whom he could not support. He appealed to Eva, "the MOTHER OF THE HUMBLE AND NEEDY, to ask for a subsidy for my family so that I can be sure that there is bread for my children, who are the future of tomorrow," and he sent along a certificate of poverty. A social report indicated that both he and his wife belonged to the Peronist Party, but again he was not accorded a pension until 1954, two years after Eva's death.[18]

Sara Morón wrote to Juan in April 1953 requesting an apartment for herself and her mother. Instead of merely petitioning for lodgings, she suggested the construction of a multistoried building with shops on the ground floor and apartments for four hundred middle- and working-class people. Sara also tried to make the plan more attractive by invoking Eva's name but insisted that the building be graced with her brother's name. He had evidently died in service to the nation, although she did not explain anything about his life.[19]

Zulema Marconi wanted to help street children in Buenos Aires by punishing their parents. Rather than arresting the children, she wanted a law that would punish severely all parents whose children were under threat of arrest. She recommended passage of a law to oblige all parents to teach their children a trade or profession. Children, if arrested by the police, should learn a trade with the help of public authorities. It is most likely that the Peronist administration did not believe this to be necessary. For them delinquent children were a thing of the past, and they had a secret study of juvenile delinquency that claimed that by 1952 the number of children arrested had declined by 25 percent since 1943. Thus this suggestion did not make its way into the second five-year plan.[20]

These are not the only surviving cases of fruitless entreaties to Juan and Eva, but they become important documents to demonstrate where the president and First Lady drew the line in political activities. While they were quite willing to intervene in very public ways that garnered them public support and notoriety, they often refrained from repeating these tactics on an everyday basis. Furthermore, Juan and Eva had to let the very slow bureaucracy take its course even when it might have cost them the personal contact so important to poor people. What, then, were Juan and Eva willing to do for people whose plights would never be heard on the news?

Patronage

The election of Juan Perón to the presidency in 1946 meant that many people had an opportunity to seek better jobs. After all, one of the hallmarks of the Radical Party was the procurement of civil-service jobs, and Peronism thus had a powerful model to follow. But most of the people who had voted for Juan came from the working class, many from provinces far from Buenos Aires. How could he funnel jobs to them? The letters written to Juan and Eva regarding job prospects show that that while many times the Peróns could intervene, they could not always control the outcome of petitions.

Irma Mirabia of La Rioja wrote Eva on January 8, 1948, seeking jobs for her mother and her sister. Initially she wished the wife of the president a happy new year and mentioned the names of prominent people who could vouch for her and her family. Then she explained the various efforts already undertaken to look for work, and finally she made her plea explaining that she had children in school and cared for an elderly father.

> For this reason I ask my good Sra. to help us. My mother is a young and capable woman, and the oldest of my half-sisters, for reasons of health and lack of resources, abandoned her studies in the third year of normal school. She has no degree but she has sufficient preparation.
>
> Two months ago positions opened in the electoral board to enroll women to vote. I ask you to intercede with the minister of the interior because all employees would remain under that ministry. She could be included there and that would resolve one part of our present situation.
>
> My lady, I have been a fervent admirer and for the past ten years, attracted by social problems, I have dedicated myself to the study of social Catholic doctrine. I am the director of the diocesan secretariat for economic and social issues, thus I think like you and General Perón. . . . If my request finds no response from you, I ask you at the very least, that you accept me as family and recognized by you. I beg you to accept my collaboration. You may send me anywhere, for God, for my Patria, and for you, I give all my energy and efforts.[21]

These entreaties must have touched the heart of the First Lady, since Eva advocated female suffrage and was quite religious. She contacted the electoral commission in La Rioja to find out if there were any jobs available, and on March 28 she received word that the electoral commission had not yet been set up, but these women would be considered for jobs when they became available. Eva's intercession was insufficient to guarantee a nonexistent job, but it might have helped them once the jobs became available.

People who wanted help placing their male relatives in better police jobs had the best luck. María del Carmen in Santa Cruz province wanted a new job for her husband. Consequently she wrote to Eva on May 4, 1950, complaining about how far away from the family her husband was stationed. A year earlier she had written to Juan Perón asking him to transfer her husband to any ministry so that he could live closer to home and help care for his elderly mother. The petition closed with a "Viva Evita y una Viva al Gral. Perón." On July 7 the minister of the interior, after several inquiries, received a note stating that the government of Santa Cruz had no problem transferring her husband. The Peróns decided nothing, as the outcome depended on the government of Santa Cruz.[22]

Similarly María Clara de Romero wrote a poignant letter to Eva asking that she help María's husband obtain a promotion after eleven years of service to the police in Río Negro. Besides stating the facts of her husband's case, María also told Eva that she came from a poor family and was studying for two careers herself. She was about to receive her degree in decorative arts despite having children and her husband. She concluded by wishing Eva and Juan the best and that she prayed that they would continue "battling for and defending the greatest destinies of our beloved country." Despite the report of the chief of police that the husband was fifth on the list for promotion on September 26, on that very day her husband received his promotion "by rigorous order according to time in office." In this case writing to Eva had stimulated the patriotism of the Río Negro police, but as seen in the prior story, there were no guarantees.[23]

Petitions for amnesty created another personal link from the president to the people. From a political perspective, however, amnesty could be very tricky for Juan Perón. As seen in chapter 5 he sometimes pardoned minors even if they didn't qualify by law. When it came to people who violated laws publically advocated by Juan as part of his Peronist strategy, they had few hopes that the president would accede to their entreaties. Such was the case of David Cantón. Dr. Tulio José Jacovella, Cantón's attorney and a federal judge, sent a telegram to the president on September 9, 1950.

As a man of the Revolution, totally identified with your Justicialista politics, and as the attorney for David Cantón, I inform you that the ministry of the interior has received a petition for a pardon from the

pena corporal [corporal punishment] my client suffers. This request was
sent on the 16th of this [*sic*] month as part of the glorious centenary of
the death of our Liberator. I now put to your consideration the date of
the Day of Atonement of the *colectividad israelita* [Jewish community].
It would be an appropriate date to concede this for a man who has done
so much for the progress of the country, as you will see in the various
written documents that are coming. I ask you to grant this pardon with
the certainty that it will be an act of justice and accept the certainty
of my personal and political devotion, along with my anticipatory
thanks.[24]

The optimistic telegram ignored glaring political realities. It did not disclose that David's plight was directly related to Perón's campaign against
price gouging and speculation. From 1947 onward, the president had gone on
the offensive with a strong consumerist campaign against inflation, a postwar reality in most of the world, and the rhetoric coincided with populist
campaigns of the times, as well as later Peronist programs in 1974. According
to Eduardo Elena, Perón had denounced businessmen who raised prices as
exhibiting "egotism, greediness, lack of human solidarity, and absence of
patriotism," and between 1945 and 1951 inflation rose sharply.[25] This campaign achieved new vigor in October 1950 when over three hundred housewives had asked the president for "collective action and boycott" against
price gougers. At that meeting Perón urged the women to cut down their
excessive consumption as he and Eva had done. He claimed to have reduced
food expenditures from 12,000 pesos per month to 1,200, a total that included
food for servants. After the meeting, police began a mass arrest of businessmen accused of speculation.[26]

Under these circumstances, David's hopes for a pardon proved to be illu-
sory. It appears that Perón never got to read the petition. Subsequent paperwork revealed that the president himself had imposed a mandatory sixty-day
house arrest according to Decree 15.503/50 for selling goods above the normal
price. David had been fined 769,845.76 pesos, a fine equal to his profit, that
remained unpaid. Furthermore, since the campaign was a personal priority
for the president, the suggestion that he should grant to pardon on the Jewish
Day of Atonement could be construed as an admission that Perón had committed a sin by promoting an antispeculation campaign. Thus Miguel

Gamboa, director general of prices and supplies, recommended against the pardon on November 9, 1950, and Perón did not grant it.

Barbers in Buenos Aires had no better luck getting special permission to raise the price of haircuts. In 1951 the Federation of Barbers and Hairdressers of the Argentine Republic, a union founded under the sponsorship of Perón himself in 1943, wrote to Juan. They claimed that the president had included them under the antispeculation Decree 36.990 of December 1948, and that

> this inclusion closes all doors to the possibility of any price increase that resulted from the rising cost of living. . . . While our profession, despite its goal to fill a high level of hygiene and beauty, the hair stylist has much of the professional and artistic in its endeavors and despite this recognition by part of our clientele, we have never been remunerated for this.[27]

They argued that there were one hundred thousand hairstylists in Argentina and that their prices did not cover their costs and "this leads to the logical conclusion that as a human consequence many professionals were leaving this line of work. . . . We neither sell nor traffic in merchandise, nor do we industrialize or sell products. We just exercise our profession." In response, three years later in 1953, bureaucrats claimed that barbers had indeed been allowed to raise their prices when the government had deemed it necessary and thus no action was taken on the request. In these cases, Perón had given bureaucrats full charge of matters related to inflation, and there was no point to sending him personal entreaties.

The letters to Juan and Eva that I have viewed basically end in 1952 for several reasons. First, Juan did not invite people to write to him regarding five-year plans after 1951. And Eva died in July 1952, thereby closing an important means of communication between the president and the people. I have cited other, later letters, but generally they prove to be exceptions. Eva's "bridge of love" had been shut down. This does not mean, however, that no letters remain from later dates. Perhaps they can be found in some of the other six hundred boxes of correspondence, and the task falls to another researcher to expand the coverage of this book. But I would argue that Eva's death put an end to many unsolicited letters for aid.

A series of petitioners after Eva's death requested free automobiles. One, addressed to Raúl Mende in April 1952, came from a member of the clergy who had Peronist Party credentials. He needed a Ford to travel throughout the rough terrain of Jujuy to fulfill his pastoral mission. In another, a physician who worked in one of the Eva Perón clinics made a similar request and noted that he had already written the First Lady. At least one of these requests, and most likely all of them, received the answer that automobiles were available in Argentina, and that the petitioners should pay the market price. The notes came from all over Argentina, from individuals as well as groups hoping that Juan would replace Eva as the "good fairy," as she had been called in the past. The Ministry of Technical Affairs did not bother to number these many requests, as Juan was not about to dispense individual favors in the same way as Eva.[28]

Indeed, the president authorized very few personal interviews or special favors even after his wife died, and he tried to put an end to the people's demands for his personal intercession that characterized Peronism during the period from 1946 to 1952. While Argentines wrote to Juan far less frequently than before, they still remembered with great fondness the meeting with Eva, the stay at the hogar de tránsito, the gifts of apple cider at Christmas, and the vacations that their children could take for the first time. These memories could never be erased, and, as time went on, they became embellished by the fond glow that often envelops pleasant remembrances of times gone by. Charisma could be established but rarely transferred, and it was not easily erased from memory. This became the difficult lesson that Argentine leaders had to face after 1955.

Conclusion

Reflections on the Enduring Nature
of Peronist Charisma

THE PRECEDING CHAPTERS certainly do not constitute a complete history of Peronism from 1946 to 1952, nor do the views found in letters to Juan and Eva claim to represent a majority view. What they show us, however, are some unique insights into the formation of charismatic bonds between the presidential couple and the unorganized poor.

Unlike members of organized working-class groups in Buenos Aires, the working poor—as well as female migrants to Buenos Aires without hopes for good employment—had few safety nets. Families back at home had usually exhausted their resources, which explains why the women and their children made their way to the capital city. The elderly rarely could move elsewhere to get help; hence the pensions given by the Peronist administration served as a literal lifeline to augment the modest resources available in their rural areas or hometown, just as the transit homes provided temporary succor to women and their offspring in Buenos Aires. Immigrants faced exactly the same realities as those born in Argentina, and by the 1940s and 1950s the welfare societies that had helped them in the past faced declining revenues and fewer members due to the popularity of labor unions for urban workers and the rise of the Eva Perón Foundation, the Eva Perón grocery stores, and the transit homes. Certainly the presence of tens of thousands of mourners from the interior who showed up at Eva's funeral testified to the bonds they felt with First Lady.

The two five-year plans served a similar function for Juan Perón. The letters that flooded the Ministry of Technical Affairs, the telegrams sent to the presidential residence, and the missives sent to Juan's brother and other high

figures in the Perón administration reassured tens of thousands of petitioners that the president knew of their plight, their dreams, their community, or
their rural location. The administration's pensions or subsidies to the rural
poor made life bearable for many, and the stories those people told social
workers provide researchers with intimate portraits of life on the edge in
Peronist Argentina.

This correspondence reaffirms the idea that Juan and Eva performed complementary roles according to gender and the particular governmental tasks
assigned to them. Juan kept in touch with the people through the five-year
plans, while Eva's meetings with the public, with women at the hogares de
tránsito, and through the Eva Perón Foundation all had different objectives.
From this perspective, Peronism could not have been as successful at cement-
ing emotional ties without Eva, and connections between individual and
community needs stated in suggestions for national planning policies
released the energies, imaginations, and hopes that people had held for many
years onto the president, Juan Perón. Children's correspondence to national
leaders through *Mundo Peronista* forged other emotive ties, ones that people
could draw upon as testimony of the caring of the Peronist years. It is this
charismatic connection that people recounted in videos at the pro-Evita
Peronist exhibition at the Palais de Glace in 1997 sponsored by the Eva Perón
Historical Association, which now can be seen at the Museo Evita housed in
one of the former hogares de tránsito. The short interviews, including the
famous and not so famous, describe Eva with great fondness. Juan simply did
not elicit those emotions, and his record depended more on the completion
of projects than the promise of favors. Yet combined, the two created lasting
charismatic bonds that can be felt even today.

Ever since Eva died in 1952 and the military removed Juan from power in
1955, Peronist politicians have tried to recapture and build upon the charisma
accrued by Juan and Eva. Juan intended to build her a mausoleum where her
plastified body could serve as the source of a cult of Eva that linked her to the
Virgin Mary. As mentioned in chapter 4, Juan enlisted a famous Spanish
embalmer, Pedro Ara, to work on her, and before she died Eva left detailed
instructions as to her hairdo, nails, lipstick, and dress. Evidently she, too,
believed that her charisma emanated from her body.

Opponents of Peronism, especially the military, became intent on prevent-
ing a cult surrounding Eva's body, and on November 23, 1955, they stole it from
her resting place at the General Confederation of Labor building. After a

circuitous journey through Buenos Aires to escape Peronists who wanted to recover it, Eva's body was eventually reburied in an Italian cemetery under a false name.[1] When it was returned to Juan at his Spanish home in Puerto de Hierro, Juan's third wife Isabela had the attic remodeled and transformed into a sanctuary for Eva. There, according to Tomás Eloy Martínez, a novelist and personal friend of the family, Juan's personal secretary José López Rega, lover of Isabela and great believer in Afro-Brazilian religious practices and magic, tried to channel Eva's charismatic powers into Isabela.[2] His attempts failed miserably, and Isabela, despite changing her hair color and style to imitate Eva, never captured Eva's popular aura or her charisma.

Juan suffered an equally ignominious fate. He died in 1974 and on June 27, 1983, robbers entered his tomb and cut off his hands—body parts that some equated with Juan's popularity and charisma. The Peronist Party refused to pay the ransom, arguing that his hands were not the source of his charisma, and they have never been returned.[3]

Since the return of democracy, Peronist politicians have continued to invoke Juan and Eva in an attempt to transfer the couple's charisma to themselves. Not surprisingly, they find themselves in the same dilemma as many politicians who want to bask in the charismatic warmth of their former leaders. In the Argentine case, these tactics have included projecting images of Juan and Eva during campaign speeches. But what images of Peronist charisma worked twenty-five years later? Carlos Saúl Menem was elected president in 1989 with a campaign that tried to imitate Juan's sex appeal. Menem portrayed himself as a star in leather pants with sideburns that changed according to his political message and had his picture published in a US magazine on his bed with a poodle, one of the symbols that identified Juan's domestic side. He later forced his wife out of the presidential palace and became known as a man with great sexual appetites.

Nestor Kirchner, Peronist candidate for president in 2003, used Photoshop techniques to create the illusion that he had been photographed with Juan and Eva. Kirchner groomed his wife, Cristina Fernández de Kirchner, to succeed him as president as Eva had wished to do. After he died suddenly in 2010, Cristina, the current president, dropped the emphasis on Juan and focused on the women of the country. She also replaced a famous general and former president (Julio Roca) with Eva's visage on the 100-peso note. Most of these efforts have failed in the long run because, as I have argued before, charismatic politics are difficult to impose from above, without input from the people, without considering women's roles, and without ideal economic conditions that can be attributed to national policy.

Argentina is not the only country that has shaped political party strategy on charismatic leaders who founded or renewed the parties they represented. In October 2010 Alexei Barrionuevo hypothesized regarding Brazil that Dilma Rousseff, then a candidate of the Workers' Party and the first Brazilian female candidate sponsored by a major party, would win the elections. However, Barrionuevo argued that Rousseff was a "political novice" who lacked "the charisma of her former boss," President Luiz Inácio Lula da Silva. He quoted the director of the Latin American Center at the University of Oxford, who opined, "This turned out to be a predictable plebiscite, a thumbs-up for the Lula years," without considering the important role women played in the emergence of democracy after years of dictatorship. The reporter did not believe Rousseff would have the "swagger" of Lula.[4] As it turned out, government corruption, the massive expenditures on the Olympics and the World Cup, and increased demands of citizens became more important than her lack of swagger or her experience of having suffered during the military dictatorship.

On March 10, 2015, William Neuman accused the current president of Venezuela, Nicolás Maduro, of imitating his predecessor Hugo Chávez too much. In the Maduro case, swagger was not enough. "Mr. Maduro came into office seeking to imitate his charismatic predecessor, in nearly every way: the way he talked, the way he dressed, and in his fulminations against American imperialism." Rather than stake out his own consensus, he simply imitated Chávez, who had died on March 5, 2013, rather than attacking the structural causes.[5] Once again gender remained invisible but implied, but this time the commentator included economic concerns.

Clearly, letter writing no longer cements leaders to their constituencies. Yet charisma still counts, even though no modern template seems to exist for creating it, nor for transferring charisma from one candidate to another. This book has shown that in the 1940s letter writing could create strong bonds, but it could not force presidents to honor all petitions from below. In contemporary politics social-media campaigns can affect leaders, but they still cannot guarantee the rich fervor that develops around a charismatic leader without taking into account issues such as gender, economics, and forms of communication.

NOTES

Introduction

1. I would like to thank Stephanie Mitchell for her observation on this nature of the charismatic bond.
2. The classic view is Weber, *On Charisma*.
3. La Fuente, *Children of Facundo*, 114.
4. Salvatore, *Wandering Paysanos*, 48–51. In the Rosas period, many women went to local authorities to demand food subsidies while their husbands were in the army or after being widowed.
5. Germani, *Política y sociedad*; Baily, *Labor, Nationalism, and Politics*; Murmis and Portantiero, *Estudios sobre los orígenes*; Corradi, "Between Corporatism and Insurgency," 109; Navarro, "Eva's Charismatic Leadership"; Di Piramo, "Charisma."
6. Blanksten, *Perón's Argentina*, 257–58.
7. Ibid., 260.
8. Ibid., ch. 5; Bianchi and Sanchis, *El Partido Peronista Femenino*, especially vol. 1.
9. Eva Perón, *La razón de mi vida*. This book has been translated into English and many other languages.
10. Cowles [María Main], *Bloody Precedent*, 152–53. Main claims that Eva's radio-station manager threatened to fire her if she didn't improvise the content and identify Juan as someone worthy of mentioning.
11. Flores, *Woman with the Whip*.
12. Ibid., 236.
13. Ibid., 237.
14. Braden, *Blue Book on Argentina*.
15. Navarro and Fraser, *Eva Perón*; Taylor, *Eva Perón*; Page, *Perón*; Plotkin,

Mañana es San Perón. See also the excellent collection on Peronist popular culture by Karush and Chamosa, *New Cultural History of Peronism*.

16. Potash, ed., *Perón y el G.O.U.*

17. Baily, *Labor, Nationalism, and Politics*; Corradi, "Between Corporatism and Insurgency," 109.

18. Di Piramo, "Charisma."

19. Ibid., 10.

20. Madsen and Snow, *Charismatic Bond*, 5, 23.

21. Chamosa, *Argentine Folklore Movement*, 157; Karush, *Culture of Class*.

22. Karush, *Culture of Class*, 178.

23. See Elena, *Dignifying Argentina*; Milanesio, *Workers Go Shopping in Argentina*.

24. Darío, *Cancionero de Juan Perón y de Eva Perón*.

25. Ibid., 107–8.

26. Juan Perón, tango lyrics, http://www.todotango.com/musica/tema/2449/Versos-de-un-payador-al-General-Juan-Peron/; Eva Perón, tango lyrics, http://www.todotango.com/musica/tema/2448/Versos-de-un-payador-a-la-senora-Eva-Peron/.

Chapter 1

1. Dueñas, *Indians and Mestizos*.

2. Guy, *Women Build the Welfare State*.

3. For more on Yrigoyen, see Horowitz, *Argentina's Radical Party*, ch. 1; Archivo Consejo Nacional de Niñez, Adolescencia y la Familia (hereafter ACNNAF), Leg. 13.633. The young man did not get either of his wishes, but the society awarded him a cash prize because of his heroism as a policeman. All names have been fictionalized.

4. For two excellent studies focusing primarily in Buenos Aires see Elena, *Dignifying Argentina*; and Milanesio, *Workers Go Shopping in Argentina*.

5. The bibliography on this topic is extensive. For examples, see Scobie, *Revolution on the Pampas*; Moya, *Cousins and Strangers*; and Sábato, *Agrarian Capitalism and the World Market*.

6. Bell, "The Jews and Perón"; Bell, "In the Name of the Community"; Rein, *Argentina, Israel y los judíos*.

7. Ministerio de Economía y Obras y Servicios Públicos, *Serie análisis demográfico 10*, 16. Omar Acha has recaptured the movement of women from the interior to a Buenos Aires neighborhood in Acha, *Crónica sentimental de la Argentina peronista*, ch. 1.

8. He had connections with the entertainment industry and eventually became Juan Perón's personal secretary until he committed suicide in 1953.

9. Navarro and Fraser, *Eva Perón*, 43. This is the earliest speech of Eva to be uncovered so far.

10. Eva Perón, *Discursos completos*, 1:9–12.

11. Navarro and Fraser, *Eva Perón*, 117.

12. ACNNAF, Leg. 58.167.

13. Néstor Ferioli, *Fundación Eva Perón*, 1:14.

14. Stated in online biography of Eva Perón at http://www.evitaperon.org/part2. htm.

15. See http://images.google.com/imgres?imgurl=http://abc.gov.ar/lainstitucion/ sistemaeducativo/educacioninicial/museoinicial/imagenes/jardin_901_ sanandresdegiles_02.jpg&imgrefurl=http://abc.gov.ar/lainstitucion/ sistemaeducativo/educacioninicial/museoinicial/historiasjardines_901_ sanandresdegiles.htm&usg=__1QCxMCqbaECoMc5D4GhQunjW1VQ=&h=22 9&w=350&sz=45&hl=en&start=20&um=1&tbnid=GB9XCV1XGxYIVM:&tbnh =79&tbnw=120&prev=/images%3Fq%3DEva%2BPeron%2B%2Bmadrina%26hl% 3Den%26rls%3Dcom.microsoft:*:IE-SearchBox%26rlz%3D1I7DKUS_ en%26um%3D1. This next anecdote relates to a mother's desire to have Eva serve as madrina, but the mother died before she could ask for the favor: http:// servicios.laverdad.es/panorama/corazonprotagonista181102.htm; http://www. noticiasnet.com.ar/?se=26&id=5375. See also http://www.taringa.net/posts/ info/937278/La-gira-de-Evita-por-Europa.html. Eva was often called the "madrina de los descamisados" (godmother of the shirtless ones).

16. Guy, *Women Build the Welfare State*, 153–56.

17. *El Laborista*, November 22, 1947, 10; November 23, 5.

18. Ibid., December 21, 1947, 3.

19. Barry, "La actividad religiosa en los hogares de tránsito," 5.

20. Barry, "Mujeres en tránsito," 85; Barry, "La actividad religiosa en los hogares de tránsito."

21. ACNNAF, Leg. 58.172.

22. ACNNAF, Leg. 60.680, February 11, 1949. The other son went to the same institution, where he remained for the same amount of time.

23. Sociedad de Damas Israelitas, *Memoria*, 1950–1951, 42.

24. ACNNAF, Leg. 58.627.

25. Archivo General de la Nación Argentina (hereafter AGN), Perón, Ministerio de Asuntos Técnicos (hereafter MAT), Caja 595.

26. ACNNAF, Leg. 64.229, September 1950.

27. ACNNAF, Leg. 58.386.

28. Many of these organizations, as well as others, had gradually been taken over by the Argentine government from the 1820s onward. Some had originally been founded by religious entities or philanthropists. People also wrote to admit their children into entities operated by the Society of Beneficence such as the Martín Rodríguez home.

29. ACNNAF, Leg. 58.969, Letter of May 3, 1948.

30. ACNNAF, Leg. 62.196.

31. ACNNAF, Leg. 64.264.

32. ACNNAF, Leg. 65.001.
33. AGN, Archivo Intermedio, Ministerio del Interior, Números Especiales, 70.000.
34. See Healy, *Ruins of the New Argentina*.
35. ACNNAF, Leg. 55.987.
36. ACNNAF, Leg. 60.060.
37. ACNNAF, Leg. 58.743.
38. ACNNAF, Leg. 58.630.
39. ACNNAF, Leg. 58.960. Federal intervention, as stated in the Argentine Constitution, allowed the chief executive to take over a variety of public and private entities and name a special person, an intervener, to take over the leadership of the organization and reform it.
40. ACNNAF, Leg. 6438. The state ultimately refused to allow this aunt to remove the children because it was feared that they would be exploited.
41. Parts of this section have been published in Guy, *Women Build the Welfare State*, ch. 6.
42. Ferioli, *Fundación Eva Perón*, 1:100; Guy, *Women Build the Welfare State*.
43. AGN, Sociedad de Beneficencia, Libro de Actas, T. 35, July 26, 1946, ff. 305–310. The quote is on f. 310; for the *La Prensa* clipping see AGN, Archivo Intermedio, Sociedad de Beneficencia, Ministerio del Interior, *La Prensa* clipping.
44. AGN, Sociedad de Beneficencia, Libro de Actas, t. 36, December 30, 1946, f. 2. Compare this with the *La Prensa* clipping.
45. *El Laborista*, "A las madres laboristas: Debe cuidarse a los hijos porque son el futuro de la patria," March 2, 1946, 7; "Al pobre le está vedado tener hijos: No le alquilan habitación a un matrimonio porque tiene dos niñitos de corta edad," April 23,1946, 6.
46. *El Laborista*, "Créose la Secretaría de Salud Pública. Designóse al Dr. Ramón Carrillo," May 30, 1946, 3; "Estudiase la adopción legal en la Argentina," June 11, 1946, 7.
47. *El Laborista*, "La Sociedad de Beneficencia no cumple con su verdadera misión," July 11, 1946, 8.
48. *El Laborista*, "'No debe ser' Sociedad de Beneficencia," August 3, 1948, 6.
49. Ibid.
50. AGN, Perón, MAT, Caja 677, Sociedad de Beneficencia de la Capital, Proyecto de Estatuto elevado por esta intervención al Sr. Secretario de Salud Pública, January 10, 1947, Cap. III, art. 7, 9. *El Laborista*, "La intervención a la Sociedad de Beneficencia debe ser urgentemente llevada a cabo con rigor. Queremos colegios, no cárceles, es lo que piden los ex-alumnos." August 4, 1946, 9; "Llegó la hora de justicia: Fue intervenida la Sociedad de Beneficencia. Rotundo Triunfo de EL LABORISTA," September 7, 1946, 1.
51. AGN, Perón, MAT, Caja 677, Sociedad de Beneficencia de la Capital, Proyecto de Estatuto elevado por esta intervención al Sr. Secretario de Salud Pública, 1947, Informe del Sr. Osorio desfavorable al proyecto presentado por la Secretaría de Salud Pública.

52. AGN, Sociedad de Beneficencia, Libro de Actas, t. 36, f. 22, December 7, 1946.

53. AGN, Sociedad de Beneficencia, Subsidios, Leg. 4, note dated September 2, 1946, from Mercedes de E. de Blaquier to President of the Society of Beneficence.

54. AGN, Sociedad de Beneficencia, Subsidios, Caja 33, Exped. 102.033. This file has a number associated with the Sociedad de Beneficencia, not with the Ministerio de Asuntos Técnicos.

55. AGN, Perón, MAT, Caja 581, Exped. 2.540.

56. Acha, *Crónica sentimental de la Argentina peronista*, ch. 3.

Chapter 2

1. Biernat and Ramacciotti, "Maternity Protection for Working Women in Argentina."

2. Guy, *Performing Charity*, ch. 6.

3. For a background of the system of charity and welfare see Guy, *Women Build the Welfare State*, especially chapters 2, 3, and 6; Subsidy Decree No. 15.515, November 6, 1946, found in *Anales de Legislación Argentina, 1946*, VI: 602–3.

4. For comments by the Society of Beneficence on its intervention see AGN, Sociedad de Beneficencia, *Libro de Actas*, t. 35, October 4, 1946, ff. 398–400. It is curious that the records of these subsidies can be found within the Sociedad de Beneficencia archives. I wish to thank Marta Goldberg and José Luis Moreno for telling me about this.

5. *El Laborista*, January 19, 1946, 7 and March 1, 1946, 4.

6. AGN, Sociedad de Beneficencia, Subsidios, 1946, Leg. 4.

7. AGN, Sociedad de Beneficencia, Subsidios, 1951, Caja 56, Leg. 65.613.

8. AGN, Perón, MAT, Leg. 599, Exped. 194/46.

9. AGN, Sociedad de Beneficencia, Subsidios, 1950, Caja 44, Leg. 107.258.

10. AGN, Sociedad de Beneficencia, Subsidios, 1948, Leg. 5.

11. AGN, Sociedad de Beneficencia, Subsidios, 1950, Caja 42, Exped. 111.780. This process took a year to complete.

12. AGN, Sociedad de Beneficencia, Subsidios, 1951, Caja 50, Exped. 74.883.

13. AGN, Sociedad de Beneficencia, Subsidios, 1950, Caja 42, Exped. 1.042.

14. AGN, Sociedad de Beneficencia, Subsidios, 1950, Caja 33, Exped. 74.929.

15. AGN, Sociedad de Beneficencia, Subsidios, 1950, Caja 44, Exped. 121.326.

16. AGN, Sociedad de Beneficencia, Subsidios, 1950, Caja 44, Leg. 115.597.

17. AGN, Sociedad de Beneficencia, Subsidios, 1950, Caja 44, Leg. 7.309.

18. AGN, Sociedad de Beneficencia, Subsidios, 1946, Leg. 4.

19. ACNNAF, Leg. 66.466.

20. AGN, Sociedad de Beneficencia, Subsidios, 1948, Leg. 5.

21. Archivo Intermedio, Ministerio del Interior Especial, 1949, Exped. 71.903. The matter was then sent to the solicitor of the treasury on August 18, 1949. No additional information exists.

22. AGN, Sociedad de Beneficencia, Subsidios, 1950, Caja 44, Exped.101.046.

23. AGN, Sociedad de Beneficencia, Subsidios, 1950, Caja 44, Exped.8.465.

24. AGN, Sociedad de Beneficencia, Subsidios, 1950, Caja 42, Exped. 11.956.

25. AGN, Sociedad de Beneficencia, Subsidios, 1950, Caja 42, Exped.4.412.

26. AGN, Sociedad de Beneficencia, Subsidios, 1950, Caja 40, Exped. 104.537.

27. AGN, Sociedad de Beneficencia, Subsidios, 1950, Caja 33, Exped. 107.719.

28. AGN, Sociedad de Beneficencia, Subsidios, 1950, Caja 44, Exped. 107.764.

29. AGN, Sociedad de Beneficencia, Subsidios, 1950, Caja 43, Exped. 120.294.

30. AGN, Sociedad de Beneficencia, Subsidios, 1950, Caja 44, Exped. 109.822.

31. AGN, Sociedad de Beneficencia, Subsidios, 1950, Caja 44, Exped. 123.714.

32. AGN, Sociedad de Beneficencia, Subsidios, 1950, Caja 44, Exped. 79.123.

33. AGN, Sociedad de Beneficencia, Subsidios, 1950, Caja 44, Exped. 122.030.

34. AGN, Sociedad de Beneficencia, Subsidios, 1950, Exped. 147.152.

35. AGN, Sociedad de Beneficencia, Subsidios, 1951, Leg. 54, Exped. 72.629.

36. AGN, Sociedad de Beneficencia, Subsidios, 1951, Leg. 54, Exped. 69.171.

37. Navarro and Fraser, *Eva Perón*, 116–17.

38. Ibid., 117–18.

39. Ibid., 124.

40. Tenti Fanfani, *Estado y pobreza*, vol. 1. Plotkin has provided the most comprehensive documentation on the foundation's funding in *Mañana es San Perón*.

41. AGN, Sociedad de Beneficencia, Subsidios, 1950, Caja 33, Leg. 121.897/50.

42. AGN, Sociedad de Beneficencia, Subsidios, 1950, Caja 33, Leg. 122.402.

43. AGN, Sociedad de Beneficencia, Subsidios, 1950, Caja 33, Leg. 101.378.

44. AGN, Sociedad de Beneficencia, Subsidios, 1950, Caja 33, Leg. 123.140.

45. AGN, Sociedad de Beneficencia, Subsidios, 1950, Caja 33, Leg. 122.854.

46. AGN, Sociedad de Beneficencia, Subsidios, 1950, Caja 35, Leg. 105.467.

47. AGN, Sociedad de Beneficencia, Subsidios, 1950, Caja 35, Leg. 101.991.

48. AGN, Sociedad de Beneficencia, Subsidios, 1950, Caja 40, Leg. 163.856.

49. AGN, Sociedad de Beneficencia, Subsidios, 1951, Caja 42, Leg. 101.179.

50. AGN, Sociedad de Beneficencia, Subsidios, 1950, Caja 43, Leg.120.294.

51. AGN, Sociedad de Beneficencia, Subsidios, 1950, Caja 43, Leg. 104.293.

52. Examples of these societies can be found in Guy, *Women Build the Welfare State*.

53. AGN, Sociedad de Beneficencia, Subsidios, 1950, Caja 44, Exped. 108.405.

54. AGN, Sociedad de Beneficencia, Subsidios, 1951, Caja 55, Exped. 72.946.

55. AGN, Sociedad de Beneficencia, Subsidios, 1951, Caja 55, Exped. 78.744.

56. AGN, Sociedad de Beneficencia, Subsidios, 1950, Exped. 126.223.

57. AGN, Sociedad de Beneficencia, Subsidios, 1951, Caja 55, Exped. 73.133.

Chapter 3

1. Elena, *Dignifying Argentina*; Milanesio, *Workers Go Shopping in Argentina.*
2. See Healy, *Ruins of the New Argentina.*
3. Elena's recent work examines the Segundo Plan Quinquenal. Elena, "What the People Want," 81–108. See also *Dignifying Argentina.*
4. *Plan Quinquenal.*
5. Juan Perón, *Obras completas,* 8:338–39.
6. *Plan Quinquenal.* On the back cover it states that the Plan Quinquenal "has reached the street due to the efforts of nine revolutionary journalists."
7. Juan Perón, *Obras Completas,* 8:343–67.
8. Ibid., 9:1, 30–31; 9:2, 440–44. *La Nación,* March 23, 1946, 1. This comment prompted further explanation from the newspaper. Throughout the month of October, *La Nación* examined many aspects of the plan.
9. *New York Times,* November 17, 1946.
10. AGN, Perón, MAT, Caja 595, no exped. number. As with all correspondence, the names of the letter writers have been changed.
11. AGN, Perón, MAT, undated, Caja 595, Exped. 2555.
12. AGN, Perón, MAT, Caja 457, Exped. 196, June 1946. This letter was originally addressed to Juan Duarte, Perón's private secretary and Eva's brother.
13. AGN, Perón, MAT, Caja 668, June 27, 1946.
14. AGN, Perón, MAT, Caja 466, Exped. 262, October 22, 1946.
15. AGN, Perón, MAT, Caja 599, Exped. 3079, November 28, 1946.
16. AGN, Perón, MAT, Caja 599, Exped. 3382, Aguilares, Tucumán, December 4, 1946.
17. AGN, Perón, MAT, Caja 547, Exped. 3840.
18. AGN, Perón, MAT, Caja 466, Exped. 128. The low number on the file indicates that it was among the first received.
19. AGN, Perón, MAT, Caja 595, November 25, 1946.
20. AGN, Perón, MAT, Caja 505. Exped. 3310, December 11, 1946.
21. AGN, Perón, MAT, Caja 597, December 24, 1947.
22. AGN, Perón, MAT, Caja 466, Exped. 3333.
23. AGN, Perón, MAT, Caja 595, Exped. 202.
24. AGN, Perón, MAT, Caja 466, Exped. 393, June 6, 1946.
25. AGN, Perón, MAT, Caja 668, June 20, 1946.
26. AGN, Perón, MAT, Caja 599, Exped. 2658, November 7, 1946.
27. AGN, Perón, MAT, Caja 668, Exped. 3044, November 22, 1946.
28. AGN, Perón, MAT, Caja 688, December 14, 1946.
29. AGN, Perón, MAT, Caja 597, Exped. 2622, October 26, 1946.
30. *La Prensa,* December 3, 1946, 11.
31. Ibid., December 10, 1946, 24.

32. AGN, Perón, MAT, Caja 597, Exped. 1419, November 6, 1948; AGN, Perón, MAT, Caja 597, Exped. 1516, November 29, 1948. It arrived at the presidential palace on December 23, 1948.

33. AGN, Perón, MAT, Caja 597, Exped. 1419.

34. AGN, Perón, MAT, Caja 597, Exped. 1562.

35. AGN, Perón, MAT, Caja 597, Exped. 1562. The judge had advocated these changes since 1943. See also Guy, *Women Build the Welfare State.*

36. *Perón cumple su Plan de Gobierno,* 37.

37. Manzano, *Age of Youth in Argentina.*

38. Partido Socialista, "Documento Político." Evidently the Socialist Party earlier published its specific criticism of the Government Plan in *El Plan Quinquenal,* already out of print by 1953.

39. Norberto Galasso, *Perón,* vol. 1, 433.

40. Patricia Barrotarán, "La planificación como instrumento," 16–17.

41. This interpretation questions, or at the very least complicates, the thesis of Maryssa Navarro, whose study of the charisma of Eva Perón reiterated the First Lady's self-perception that she was the facilitator, the "bridge of love," between Juan and the people. Navarro, "Eva's Charismatic Leadership."

42. Acha, "Sociedad civil y sociedad política."

43. See Navarro, "The Case of Eva Perón" and "Evita and the Crisis of 17 October 1945," which discuss Eva's early involvement in politics. Taylor, *Eva Perón,* analyzes these myths from a class and gendered perspective.

Chapter 4

1. Juan Perón, *Obras completas,* 14:2, 608–10.

2. Brennan and Rougier, *Politics of National Capitalism,* 41–54.

3. AGN, Perón, MAT, Caja 150, Exped. 18.708.6.

4. Elena, "What the People Want," 82. See also Elena, "Peronist Consumer Politics"; Milanesio, "'Guardian Angels of the Domestic Economy.'"

5. This chapter does not claim to represent the typical letter, most of which were about public works, schools, and other plans; rather, letters were selected to show how letter writing cemented political affiliations and how some believe they could influence bureaucracy in this way.

6. Eva Perón, *Discursos completos,* 2:355.

7. Juan Perón, *Obras completas,* 14:2, "Primera charla," November 3, 1951, 687.

8. Lerner, "The Illness and Death of Eva Perón." See also Navarro and Fraser, *Eva Perón.*

9. AGN, Perón, MAT, Caja 457, February 15, 1951.

10. Navarro and Fraser, *Eva Perón,* ch. 9.

11. Ibid., 137.

12. Eva Perón, *Evita in My Own Words*, 90. See also the extensive introduction.
13. ACNNAF, Legs. 6312–13.
14. Guy, "Life and the Commodification of Death in Argentina."
15. AGN, Asuntos Técnicos, Caja 457, Exped. 5282.
16. *Mundo Peronista*, 4, no. 75 (November 1, 1954): 38.
17. *Cancionero de Perón y Eva Perón.*
18. AGN, Perón, MAT, Leg. 18.706.
19. AGN, Perón, MAT, Caja 342, Exped. 5.249.
20. AGN, Perón, MAT, Caja 43, Exped. 5.371; Caja 69, Exped. 6.282, December 10, 1951.
21. AGN, Perón, MAT, Caja 342, Exped. 15.709. No response included.
22. AGN, Perón, MAT, Caja 43, Exped. 15.506; See Hugo Klappenbach, "Historia de la orientación profesional en Argentina."
23. AGN, Perón, MAT, Caja 342, Exped. 8.283.
24. AGN, Perón, MAT, Caja 69, Exped. 10.399.
25. AGN, Perón, MAT, Caja 342, Exped. 5.249, December 4, 1951; AGN, Perón, MAT, Caja 342, Exped. 5.552, December 6, 1951.
26. AGN, Perón, MAT, Caja 150, Exped. 7.330.
27. AGN, Perón, MAT, Caja 342, Exped. 8.647.
28. AGN, Perón, MAT, Caja 4, Exped. 9.644, December 21, 1951.
29. AGN, Perón, MAT, Caja 69, Exped. 8.062.
30. AGN, Perón, MAT, Caja 69, Exped. 9650, December 1951.
31. AGN, Perón, MAT, Caja 43, Exped. 14.934, Sarandi, December 9, 1951.
32. AGN, Perón, MAT, Caja 342, Exped. 683.822, December 9, 1946.
33. AGN, Perón, MAT, Caja 342, Exped. 17.854.
34. AGN, Perón, MAT, Caja 342, Exped. 16.723. No date.
35. AGN, Perón, MAT, Caja 342, Exped. 13.220, December 21, 1951.
36. AGN, Perón, MAT, Caja 342, Exped.18.152, January 27, 1952.
37. AGN, Perón, MAT, Caja 150, Exped. 18.772.
38. AGN, Perón, MAT, Caja 595, Exped. 1.825. The author lived in downtown Buenos Aires. The author received a note from the Ministry of Technical Affairs acknowledging receipt of his proposal.
39. AGN, Perón, MAT, Caja 342, Exped. 10.331. The author, from San Juan province, bombarded the president with his requests.
40. AGN, Perón, MAT, Caja 342, Exped. 7.931.
41. AGN, Perón, MAT, Caja 457, no exped. number.
42. AGN, Perón, MAT, Caja 69, Exped. 108.44, undated.
43. AGN, Perón, MAT, Caja 599, Exped. 8031, December 28, 1951.
44. AGN, Perón, MAT, Caja.69, Exped. 6.282, December 10, 1951.
45. AGN, Perón, MAT, Caja 342, Exped. 1.7656, January 30, 1952.
46. AGN, Perón, MAT, Caja 150. Exped. 9424.
47. AGN, Perón, MAT, Caja 581, 1.969. The files in these boxes all have numbering

that should be much larger given the date. This raises questions about how the numbers for the expedientes were allocated.

48. AGN, Perón, MAT, Caja 581, Exped. 2058, February 15, 1953. This letter was written to Juan Duarte, the president's personal secretary, and on the original letter there was a notation in red: "*interesante leer*" (interesting to read).

49. AGN, Perón, MAT, Caja 581, Exped. 793, January 29, 1953.

50. AGN, Perón, MAT, Caja 581, Exped. 3.110.

51. Catalan, "Protection Revisited." See also Jenkins, *Dependent Industrialization in Latin America*, and García Heras, *Automotores norteamericanos*.

52. AGN, Perón, MAT, Caja 595, Exped. 832. Included were blueprints of the automobile design.

53. AGN, Perón, MAT, Caja 594, Exped. 1125.

54. Ibid., Exped. 1812.

55. Ibid., Exped. 1477.

56. AGN, Perón, MAT, Caja 645, Exped. 8414. The author of the invention that dealt with public lighting was actually her first husband, and her second husband had recently died without a pension after forty years of labor.

57. AGN, MAT, Caja 580.

58. Ianantuoini, *El Segundo Plan Quinquenal*, 1.

59. Ibid., 4.

Chapter 5

1. Meyer Arana, *La caridad en Buenos Aires*, I: 372–73.

2. Sociedad de Beneficencia, *Memorias*, 1900, 153–254. At that time the Boys' Orphanage was the only place in Buenos Aires where minors were instructed in military training.

3. AGN, Defensoría de Menores, Memoria 1894, T. 1, Sección Norte, 139. Ministerio de Justicia, Leg. 112, Letra D., Manuscript of Annual Report of Defensores de Menores, Report of Defensor Castellanos, April 9, 1912.

4. See AGN, Sociedad de Beneficencia, Leg. 163, f. 194, Director General de Arsenales de Guerra to the Sociedad de Beneficencia, April 19, 1915, and f. 195, April 23, 1915.

5. Patronato de la Infancia, Libro de Actas, Libro 2, 1894–1897, ff. 35, October 10, 1894; 156 Statutes of Escuela de Artes y Oficios, June 3, 1896.

6. Patronato de la Infancia, *Memoria*, 1908–1909, 20–21.

7. Patronato de la Infancia, *Anales del Patronato de la Infancia* (1914), 14–16.

8. http://www.eldia.com.ar/especiales/proceres/n8.htm; http://www.nuevociclo.com.ar/unpalacio.htm.

9. AGN, Ministerio de Justicia e Instrucción Pública (FMJIP), Leg. 105, November 21, 1905, letter of Defender J. M. Terrero to Minister of Justice Antonio Bermejo.

10. *Reglamento Provisorio*, 3; Art. 61–63, 19.

11. Letter from Ramón Domínguez to Minister of Justice R. Naón, AGN, Leg. 110, March 31, 1909. When officials found a place for Domingo, they discovered that the father had given an inaccurate address.

12. AGN, FMJIP, Letra P, Leg. 375.

13. *El Laborista*, July 17, 1947, 2.

14. All names of parents and children have been fictionalized. ACNNAF, Leg. 58.632.

15. ACNNAF, March 27, 1944, Leg. 60.702.

16. The Patronato Nacional de Menores handled mostly delinquent children, but in their schools and reformatories they mixed delinquents with street children and those turned in by their parents.

17. ACNNAF, Leg. 62431, December 23, 1947.

18. ACNNAF, Leg. 60.131, January 3, 1947. This letter was probably misdated, as Eva did not go to Spain until 1947. For this reason I have changed the date to 1948.

19. AGN, Perón, MAT, Exped. 60.272, Presidencia Roque Saénz Peña, February 9, 1948.

20. ACNNAF, Leg. 61721.

21. AGN, Perón, Asuntos Técnicos, Exped. 65.572, Armando F. of Córdoba to Eva Perón, May 5, 1949.

22. Ibid.

23. See Guy, *Women and the Welfare State*, ch. 4.

24. ACNNAF, Leg. 62.108.

25. ACNNAF, Leg. 62.078.

26. ACNNAF, Leg. 59410. Letter from Anita Piccardo to Eva Perón, July 9, 1949.

27. ACNNAF, Leg. 63443, October 9, 1949.

28. ACNNAF, Leg. 64820.

29. Ibid.

30. ACNNAF, Leg. 64290, January 23, 1950.

31. Ibid., letter of March 6, 1950.

32. ACNNAF, Leg. 64.835.

33. ACNNAF, Leg. 64.820.

34. Ibid.

35. Ibid.

36. AGN, Decretos P. E. N. Decree 17.252, August 16, 1950.

37. ACNNAF, Leg. 60.686.

38. ACNNAF, Leg. 62.502.

Chapter 6

1. AGN, Sociedad de Beneficencia, Subsidios, 1946, Leg. 4.

2. Elena, *Dignifying Argentina*, 144–45.

3. Argentina, *El libro negro*.
4. AGN, Archivo Intermedio, Ministerio del Interior Especial, 1949, Leg. 70.019.
5. AGN, Archivo Intermedio, Ministerio del Interior Especial, 1949, Leg. 21.042.
6. AGN, Archivo Intermedio, Ministerio del Interior Especial, 1949, Leg. 70.031, January 31, 1949.
7. AGN, Archivo Intermedio, Ministerio del Interior Especial, 1949, Leg. 70.884.
8. AGN, Archivo Intermedio, Ministerio del Interior Especial, 1949, Exped. 70838, San Juan, March 31, 1949.
9. AGN, Archivo Intermedio, Ministerio del Interior Especial, 1949, Leg. 70.800.
10. AGN, Archivo Intermedio, Ministerio del Interior Especial, 1949, Leg. 7.522.
11. Archivo Intermedio, Ministerio del Interior Especial, 1949, Leg. 70.551. This file contains a series of letters written to Juan and Eva about problems associated with the earthquake.
12. AGN, Archivo Intermedio, Ministerio del Interior Especial, 1949, Leg. 71.291.
13. AGN, Archivo Intermedio, Ministerio del Interior Especial, 1950, Leg. 71.861. The name on the cover is different from the person who signed the letter.
14. AGN, Archivo Intermedio, Ministerio del Interior Especial, 1950, Leg. 71.968.
15. AGN, Sociedad de Beneficencia, Subsidios, 1948, Leg. 8, Exped. 31.477.
16. AGN, Sociedad de Beneficencia, Subsidios, 1950, Leg. 33, Exped. 75.105.
17. AGN, Sociedad de Beneficencia, Subsidios, Leg. 44, Exped. 5.717.
18. AGN, Sociedad de Beneficencia, Subsidios, Leg. 1951, Exped. 80.255.
19. AGN, Perón, MAT, Caja 341.
20. AGN, Perón, MAT, Caja 342, Presidencia de la Nación, Ministerio de Asuntos Técnicos, *Servicio Estadístico Oficial de la República Argentina, La delincuencia infantil en la Capital Federal. Boletín Diario Secreto*, No. 608, August 8, 1952, 1.
21. AGN, Archivo Intermedio, Ministerio del Interior Especial, 1949, Exped. 70.032, Letra M.
22. AGN, Archivo Intermedio, Ministerio del Interior Especial, 1949, Exped. 7.165, 1950.
23. Archivo Intermedio, Ministerio del Interior Especial, 1949, Exped. 71.870, July 26, 1950.
24. AGN, Archivo Intermedio, Ministerio del Interior Especial, Exped. 71872.
25. Quoted in Elena, "Peronist Consumer Politics," 111.
26. "Argentina, Advice for Housewives," *Time*, October 16, 1950.
27. AGN, Perón, MAT, Leg. 342, Exped. 12.534, December 20, 1951.
28. AGN, Perón, MAT, Caja 595. These have all been gathered into a group without any file numbers.

Conclusion

1. Ara, *El caso Eva Perón*. For more details see Guy, "Life and the Commodification of Death."

2. Eloy Martínez, *Perón Novel*, 252–55. According to the author, this was done to ensure Isabela's power as well as the magician's power over her.

3. Guy, "Life and the Commodification of Death."

4. *New York Times*, October 3, 2010, A10.

5. Ibid., October 3, 2015.

BIBLIOGRAPHY

Archival Sources

Archivo Consejo Nacional de la Niñez, Adolescencia y la Familia (ACNNAF)
Archivo General de la Nación Argentina (AGN)
  Defensoría de Menores
  Fondo Ministerio de Justicia e Instrucción Pública (FMJIP)
  Fondo Perón, Ministerio de Asuntos Técnicos (MAT)
  Fondo Sociedad de Beneficencia
    —Libro de Actas
    —Subvenciones
Archivo Intermedio
  Fondo Ministerio del Interior Especial

Newspapers and Magazines

Anales de Legislación Argentina
El Laborista
Mundo Peronista
New York Times
Time magazine

Primary Sources

Argentina. Comisión Nacional de Investigación. *El libro negro de la segunda tiranía.* Buenos Aires: Edición Integración. 1958.
Cancionero de Perón y Eva Perón. Buenos Aires: Grupo Editor de Buenos Aires, 1966.

"The Day Which Split History: October 17, 1945." http://www.evitaperon.org/part2.htm.

La gira de Evita por Europa. http://www.taringa.net/posts/info/937278/La-gira-de-Evita-por-Europa.html.

Márquez Piquer, Concha. http://servicios.laverdad.es/panorama/corazonprotagonista181102.htm.

Ministerio de Economía y Obras y Servicio Públicos. Secretaría de Política Económica, Instituto Nacional de Estadística y Censos. *Situación demográfica 10.* Buenos Aires: INDEC, 1997.

Patronato de la Infancia. Libro de Actas, Libro 2, 1894–1897, ff. 35, October 10, 1894; 156 Statutes of Escuela de Artes y Oficios, June 3, 1896.

Perón, Eva. *Discursos completos.* 6 volumes. Buenos Aires: Privately printed. 1965.

———. *Evita in My Own Words: The Controversial "Deathbed Manuscript" Attributed to Eva Perón with an Introduction by Joseph A. Page.* Translated by Joseph A. Page. New York: The New Press, 1966.

———. *La razón de mi vida.* Buenos Aires: Ediciones Relevo, 1973.

Perón, Juan. *Obras completas.* 27 volumes. Buenos Aires: Fundación pro Universidad de la Producción y del Trabajo; Fundación Universidad a Distancia "Hernandarias," 1977.

Plan Quinquenal de Gobierno del Presidente Perón, 1947–1951. Buenos Aires: Editorial Primicias, 1950.

Presidencia de la Nación, Ministerio de Asuntos Técnicos, *Servicio Estadístico Oficial de la República Argentina. La delincuencia infantil en la Capital Federal. Boletín Diario Secreto:608 (8 agosto),* 1952.

Reglamento Provisorio de la Casa de Corrección de Menores Varones de la Capital. Buenos Aires: La Defensa, 1899.

Segundo Plan Quinquenal de la Nación Argentina. Buenos Aires: Hechos e Ideas, 1954.

Sociedad de Damas Israelitas. *Memoria, 1950–1951.* Buenos Aires: n.p., n.d.

Todo Tango. "Versos de un payador a la Señora Eva Perón." http://www.todotango.com/musica/tema/2448/Versos-de-un-payador-a-la-senora-Eva-Peron/.

———. "Versos de un payador al General Juan Perón." http://www.todotango.com/musica/tema/2449/Versos-de-un-payador-al-General-Juan-Peron/.

Secondary Sources

Acha, Omar. *Crónica sentimental de la Argentina peronista: Sexo, inconsciente e ideología, 1945–1955.* Buenos Aires: Prometeo Libros, 2014.

———. "Sociedad civil y sociedad política durante el primer peronismo." *Desarrollo Económico; Revista de Ciencias Sociales* 44, no. 174 (July–September 2004), 199–230.

Ara, Pedro. *El caso Eva Perón (Apuntes para la historia)*. Buenos Aires: CVS Editores, 1974.

Baily, Samuel L. *Labor, Nationalism, and Politics in Argentina*. New Brunswick, NJ: Rutgers University Press, 1967. Chicago, IL: University of Chicago Press, 1953.

Barrotarán, Patricia ."La planificación como instrumento: Políticas y organización en el estado peronista (1946–1949)." In *Sueños de bienestar en la Nueva Argentina; Estado y políticas públicas durante el peronismo 1946–1955*, edited by Patricia Barrotarán, Aníbal Jáuregui, and Marcelo Rougier, 15–46. Buenos Aires: Imago Mundi, 2004.

Barrotarán, Patricia, Aníbal Jáuregui, and Marcelo Rougier, eds. *Sueños de bienestar en la Nueva Argentina: Estado y políticas públicas durante el peronismo 1946–1955*. Buenos Aires: Imago Mundi, 2004.

Barry, Carolina. "La actividad religiosa en los hogares de tránsito de la Fundación Eva Perón: Las Hermanas del Huerto." *VII Jornadas de Historia de la Iglesia*. www.uca.edu.ar/esp/sec-fteologia/images/jh/barry_hermanas.pdf, 5.

———. "La actividad religiosa en los hogares de tránsito de la Fundación Eva Perón: Las Hermanas del Huerto." *VIII Jornadas de Historia de la Iglesia*. http://culturauca.com.ar/esp/sec-fteologia/images/jh/barry_hermanas.pdf.

———. "Mujeres en tránsito." In *La Fundación Eva Perón y las mujeres: Entre la provocación y la inclusión*, edited by Carolina Barry, Karina Ramacciotti, and Adriana Valobra, 77–117. Buenos Aires: Editorial Biblos, 2008.

Bell, Lawrence, "The Jews and Perón: Communal Politics and National Identity in Peronist Argentina, 1946–55." PhD diss., Ohio State University, 2002.

———. "In the Name of the Community: Populism, Ethnicity and Politics among the Jews of Argentina, 1946–1955." *Hispanic American Historical Review* 86, no. 1 (2006): 93–122.

Bianchi, Susana, and Norma Sanchis. *El Partido Peronista Femenino*. 2 vols. Buenos Aires: Editorial Centro Editor, 1988.

Biernat, Carolina, and Karina Ramacciotti, "Maternity Protection for Working Women in Argentina: Legal and Administrative Aspects in the First Half of the Twentieth Century." http://www.scielo.br/pdf/hcsm/v18s1/en_09.pdf.

Blanksten, George. *Perón's Argentina*. Chicago, IL: University of Chicago Press, 1953.

Braden, Spruille. *Blue Book on Argentina: Consultation among American Republics with Respect to the Argentina Situation. Memorandum of the US Government*. Washington, DC: US Department of State, 1946.

Brennan, James P., and Marcelo Rougier. *The Politics of National Capitalism: Peronism and the Argentine Bourgeoisie, 1946–76*. University Park: Pennsylvania State University Press, 2009.

Catalan, Jordi. "Protection Revisited: The Development of the Automobile Industry in Argentina, Spain and South Korea, 1945–87." http://www.ekh.lu.se/ehes/paper/catalanundtext6%20(2).pdf.

Chamosa, Oscar. *The Argentine Folklore Movement: Sugar Elites, Criollo Workers, and the Politics of Cultural Nationalism, 1900–1955*. Tuscon: University of Arizona Press, 2010.

Corradi, Juan, "Between Corporatism and Insurgency: The Sources of Ambivalence in Peronist Ideology." In *Terms of Conflict: Ideology in Latin American Politics*, edited by Morris J. Blachman and Ronald G. Hellman, 97–127. New York: Random House, 1952.

Cowles, Fleur [María Main]. *Bloody Precedent*. New York: Random House, 1952.

Darío Alessandro, Julio, director. *Cancionero de Juan Perón y de Eva Perón: Realizado por un equipo de G. E. de B. A. bajo la dirección de Julio Darío Alessandro*. Buenos Aires: Grupo Editor de Buenos Aires, 1966.

Di Piramo, Daniela. "Charisma, Political Innovation and Why Superman is Rational: The Case of Argentina's Juan Perón." *Estudios Interdisciplinarios*. http://www.tasa.org.au/conferences/conferencepapers04/docs/THEORY/DI_PIRAMO.pdf.

Dueñas, Alcira. *Indians and Mestizos in the "Lettered City": Reshaping Justice, Social Hierarchy, and Political Culture in Colonial Peru*. Boulder: University of Colorado Press, 2010.

Elena, Eduardo. *Dignifying Argentina: Peronism, Citizenship, and Mass Consumption*. Pittsburgh, PA: Pittsburgh University Press, 2011.

———. "Peronist Consumer Politics and the Problem of Domesticating Markets in Argentina, 1943–1955." *Hispanic American Historical Review* 87, no. 1 (2007): 245–72.

———. "What the People Want: State Planning and Political Participation Peronist Argentina, 1946–1955." *Journal of Latin American Studies* 37: 81–108.

Eloy Martínez, Tomás. *The Perón Novel*. New York: Pantheon Press, 1988.

Ferioli, Néstor. *La Fundación Eva Perón*. 2 volumes. Buenos Aires: Centro Editor de América Latina, 1990.

Flores, María. *The Woman with the Whip: Eva Perón*. New York: Doubleday, 1952.

Galasso, Norberto. *Perón: Formación, ascenso y caída (1893–1955)*. Vol. 1. Buenos Aires: Ediciones Colihue, 2005.

García Heras, Raúl. *Automotores norteamericanos, caminos y modernización urbana en la Argentina, 1918–1939*. Buenos Aires: Libros de Hispanoamérica, 1985.

Germani, Gino. *Política y sociedad en una época de transición*. Mexico City: Paidós, 1966.

Guy, Donna J. "Life and the Commodification of Death in Argentina: Juan and Eva Perón." In *Death, Dismemberment, and Memory: Body Politics in Latin America*, edited by Lyman L. Johnson, 245–72. Albuquerque: University of New Mexico Press, 2004.

———. *Women Build the Welfare State: Performing Charity and Creating Rights in Argentina, 1880–1955*. Durham, NC: Duke University Press, 2009.

Healy, Mark A. *The Ruins of the New Argentina: Peronism and the Remaking of San Juan after the 1944 Earthquake.* Durham, NC: Duke University Press, 2011.

Horowitz, Joel. *Argentina's Radical Party and Popular Mobilization, 1916–1930.* University Park: Pennsylvania State University Press, 2009.

Ianantuoini, Domingo Rafael. *El Segundo Plan Quinquenal al Alcance de los Niños de acuerdo con el programa de educación primaria de los grados quinto y sexto de las escuelas del país.* Buenos Aires: Editorial Luis Lasserre, 1953.

Jenkins, Rhys Owen. *Dependent Industrialization in Latin America: The Automotive Industry in Argentina, Chile, and Mexico.* New York: Praeger, 1976.

Johnson, Lyman J., ed. *Death, Dismemberment, and Memory: Body Politics in Latin America.* Albuquerque: University of New Mexico Press, 2004.

Karush, Matthew B. *Culture of Class: Radio and Cinema and the Making of a Divided Argentina, 1920–1946.* Durham, NC: Duke University Press.

Karush, Matthew B., and Oscar Chamosa, eds. *The New Cultural History of Peronism: Power and Identity in Mid-Twentieth-Century Argentina.* Durham, NC: Duke University Press, 2010.

Klappenbach, Hugo. "Historia de la orientación profesional en Argentina." *Orientación y Sociedad* 5 (2005). http://www.scielo.org.ar/pdf/orisoc/v5/v5a03.pdf/, accessed on July 26, 2010.

La Fuente, Ariel de. *Children of Facundo: Caudillo and Gaucho Insurgency during the Argentine State Formation Process (La Rioja, 1853–1870).* Durham, NC: Duke University Press, 2000.

Lerner, Barron H. "The Illness and Death of Eva Perón: Cancer, Politics, and Secrecy." *Lancet* 355 (June 3, 2000): 1988–1991.

Madsen, Douglas, and Peter G. Snow. *The Charismatic Bond: Political Behavior in Times of Crisis.* Cambridge, MA: Harvard University Press, 1991.

Manzano, Valeria. *The Age of Youth in Argentina: Culture, Politics, and Sexuality from Perón to Videla.* Chapel Hill: University of North Carolina Press, 2014.

Meyer Arana, Alberto. *La caridad en Buenos Aires.* 2 vols. Buenos Aires: Imprenta Sopena, 1911.

Milanesio, Natalia. "'The Guardian Angels of the Domestic Economy': Housewives' Responsible Consumption in Peronist Argentina." *Journal of Women's History* 18, no. 3 (2006): 91–117.

———. *Workers Go Shopping in Argentina: The Rise of Popular Consumer Culture.* Albuquerque: University of New Mexico Press, 2013.

Moya, José. *Cousins and Strangers: Spanish Immigrants in Argentina, 1850–1930.* Berkeley: University of California Press, 1998.

Murmis, Miguel, and Juan Carlos Portantiero. *Estudios sobre los orígenes del peronismo.* Buenos Aires: Siglo XXI, 1971.

Navarro, Maryssa. "The Case of Eva Perón." *Signs* 3, no. 1 (Autumn 1977): 229–40.

———. "Eva's Charismatic Leadership," in *Latin American Leaders in Comparative Perspective*, edited by Michael L. Conniff. Albuquerque: University of New Mexico Press, 1982.

———. "Evita and the Crisis of 17 October 1945: A Case Study of Peronist and Anti-Peronist Mythology" *Journal of Latin American Studies* 12, no. 1 (May 1980): 127–38.

Navarro, Maryssa, and Nicholas Fraser. *Eva Perón*. New York: W. W. Norton, 1980.

Page, Joseph A. *Perón: A Biography*. New York: Random House, 1983.

Partido Socialista Argentina. *El Segundo Plan Quinquenal*. Buenos Aires: Casa del Pueblo, 1953.

Perón cumple su Plan de Gobierno: "Mejor que decir es hacer y mejor que prometer es realizar." Buenos Aires: Guillermo Kraft, 1948.

Plan Quinquenal de Gobierno del Presidente Perón, 1947–1951. Buenos Aires: Editorial Primicias, 1950.

Plotkin, Mariano Ben. *Mañana es San Perón: Propaganda, rituales políticos y educación en el régimen peronista (1946–1955)*. Buenos Aires: Ariel Historia Argentina, 1994.

Potash, Robert, ed. *Perón y el G.O.U.: Los documentos de una logia secreta*. Buenos Aires: Editorial Sudamericana, 1984.

Rein, Ranaan. *Argentina, Israel y los judíos: Encuentros y desencuentros, mitos y realidades*. Buenos Aires: Lumière, 2001.

Sábato, Hilda. *Agrarian Capitalism and the World Market: Buenos Aires in the Pastoral Age, 1840–1890*. Albuquerque: University of New Mexico Press, 1990.

Salvatore, Ricardo D. *Wandering Paysanos: State Order and Subaltern Experience in Buenos Aires During the Rosas Era*. Durham, NC: Duke University Press, 2003.

Scobie, James. *Revolution on the Pampas: A Social History of Argentine Wheat 1860–1910*. Austin: University of Texas Press, 1964.

Taylor, Julie M. *Eva Perón: The Myths of a Woman*. Chicago, IL: University of Chicago Press, 1979.

Tenti Fanfani, Emilio. *Estado y pobreza: Estrategias típicas de intervención*. 2 vols. Buenos Aires: Centro Editor de América Latina, 1989.

Weber, Max. *On Charisma and Institution Building*. Edited by S. N. Eisenstadt. Chicago, IL: University of Chicago Press, 1968.

INDEX

The letter *c* or *n* following a page number indicates a chart or note on the cited page(s). The number following the *n* refers to the note number.

Abel (letter writer), 38

Acha, Omar, 39, 148n7

Aguilla, Ramón (letter writer), 97

Akbar, Ahmed (letter writer), 132–33

Alessandro, Julio Darío, 9

Alonso, Pilar and María C. (letter writers), 74–75

Alsina, María (letter writer), 112–14

Amelia (letter writer), 135–36

Antonini, Enriqueta (letter writer), 56

Ara, Pedro, 89, 144

Archivo Intermedio, 131

Arenaza, Carlos de, 113

Argentine Blue Book, 5

Argentine Institute for the Promotion of Trade, 85

Argentine National Archive, 8

Argentine National Council on the Child, Adolescent and Family (ACNNAF), 8

Argentine Socialist Party, 82–83

Argentine Union of Intellectual Workers, 75

Aros Romana, Eliana de (letter writer), 72–73

Arroyo, Ramonda de (letter writer), 60–61

Asta, Maria Melo de (letter writer), 46–48

Automotores Argentino, 102

Avellaneda, Nicolás, minister of education, 13–14

Bagnatti, Pedro R. (letter writer), 126

Baily, Samuel, 6

Balán, Edelina Orso de (letter writer), 24

Baroni, Mr. A. (letter writer), 75–76

Barrionuevo, Alexei (letter writer), 146

Benítez, Father, 5

Berrotarán, Patricia, 83

Bianchi, Andrés (letter writer), 132

Blanksten, George, 3–4

Borlenghi, Ángel, 131

Braden, Spruille, 5

Brennan, James, 6

Briano, Carlos (letter writer), 90–91

"bridge of love". *See under* Perón, Eva
    Duarte de
Brione, Elvira, 56–57, 59
Buenos Aires, 1936 male and female
    population and, 17c
Buenos Aires, 1947 male and female
    population and, 17c
Buenos Aires, male and female migra-
    tion and, 16c

Cano, José (letter writer), 89
Canseco, Olivia (letter writer), 57–58
Carena, José (letter writer), 26–27
Carillo, Ramón, 22–23
Carmen, María del (letter writer), 139
Carmen Sula, Maria del (letter writer),
    57
Castro, Adriana de (letter writer), 26
Castro, Lt. Col., 26–27
Castro, Sra. Jacinta (letter writer), 108
Chamosa, Oscar, 7–8
charisma: "charismatic bond" and, 7;
    concept of, 1–2; early studies of,
    3; economics and, 146; forms of
    communication and, 146; gender
    roles and, 146
charitable organizations, 10, 28–29,
    149n28; Child Protection Society
    (Patronato de la Infancia) and,
    109–10; Ladies of St. Vincent de
    Paul and, 29–30; Patriotic
    Schools and, 109; Peronist wel-
    fare state and, 29; unions and,
    41–42. *See also* Moreno, Fran-
    cisco P.; Society of Beneficence
Ciano, Samuel (letter writer), 102
Colmenar, Juan (letter writer), 57
Comaro, José Jesús (letter writer), 64
Consejo Nacional de Niños, 115
Contini, Marta Catalina de (letter
    writer), 54–55
Corradi, Juan, 6

Correa, Juan (letter writer), 135
Correctional Home for Minor Boys of
    the National Capital, 110
Cowles, Fleur. *See* Main, María (Fleur
    Cowles)
Cuenta, María (letter writer), 27–28

Dacosta, Elena (letter writer), 91
Dante, Eduardo (letter writer), 76
Decker, Rudolfo A. national deputy, 22
Decree No. 15.515, Charitable Subsidies,
    65
Democracia, La, 19, 21
Desnate, Roberto, 73–74
Domínguez, Ramón (letter writer), 110
Donatti, Lorenza (letter writer), 96
Duarte, Eva: first radio speech, 1946, 19;
    Perón, Juan and, 18; radio and
    motion pictures and, 18. *See also*
    Perón, Eva Duarte de
Duarte, Juan, 18, 130, 148n3

"elderly" definitions, 46
Elena, Eduardo, 86, 131
Elena, Eduardo (letter writer), 140–41
El libro negro de la segunda tiranía, 131
Eloisa, Miguel (letter writer), 90
Entre Ríos, Lidia, 53
Escuelas Patrias, 109
Eva Perón (Fraser, Navarro), 5
Eva Perón Foundation: applicants' dig-
    nity and, 65; bureaucratic wel-
    fare state and, 59; Ciudad
    Infantil Armanda Allen and, 93;
    Department of Social Assistance
    and, 44; Eva's death and, 89;
    incorporation of, 58; letters to,
    20–21; pensions and, 42–43;
    Perón, Juan and, 65; requests for
    subsidies and, 64–65; Secretariat
    of Labor and Welfare and, 49;
    the unemployed and, 61

Eva Perón: Myths of a Woman (Taylor), 5–6

F., Armando (letter writer), 117–18
Fanfani, Emilio Tenti, 59
Federation of Barbers and Hairdressers of the Argentine Republic, 141
Felippa, Arsenio (letter writer), 91–92
Ferioli, Nestor, 21
Ferrero, Andrés (letter writer), 125–26
Florencia (letter writer), 31
Flores, María, 5
Franco, Graciela de (letter writer), 111
Fraser, Nicholas, 19, 59–60; *Eva Perón*, 5
Fresco, Manuel, 32–33
Fuente, Ariel de la, 2
Fuentes, Ricardo (letter writer), 93
Fuerte, Manuel (letter writer), 96

Galasso, Norberto, 83
Gamboa, Miguel, 141
Garcia, Graciela (letter writer), 31
Garena, Pablo, 81–82
Garza, Adelina (letter writer), 96
Garza, Alfonso (letter writer), 102
General Confederation of Labor, 70
Gianini, Carlos, 91
Gil, Eduardo, 121–22
Gorman, María de, 70; *Veinte años perdidos* and, 70–71
Gormendi, Juan (letter writer), 122–23
Goyena, Pablo (letter writer), 133–34
Graf, Elida Nedina de (petitioner), 22
Greek baby (letter), 30–31
Grupo Editor de Buenos Aires, 9
Guillermo, Florencia de (letter writer), 116–17
Guiso, Leandra de (letter writer), 131
Gutiérrez, Omar (letter writer), 125

inflation: consumers and, 97, 140; first five-year plan and, 85–86;

foreign exchange and, 83; pensions, subsidies and, 43, 90–91; post WW II and, 96, 140; provincial governments and, 14–15; renters, homeowners and, 96; Segundo Plan Quinquenal and, 86, 87, 105
Institute for Social Welfare, 36
Instituto de Colonos, 71

Jacovella, Tulio José (letter writer), 139
James, Daniel, 6
Jensen, Adela Candiani de, 24
Jewish women, 24–25
Justo, Agustín P., president, 27, 28

Kabbi, Regina B. (letter writer), 114–15
Kaiser, Henry, 102
Karush, Matthew B., 8
Kaufman, Julia Noriega de (letter writer), 25
Kirchner, Cristina Fernández de, 145
Kirchner, Nestor, 145

Laborista, El, 21, 44; antibiotics and, 22; on welfare state, 34–35
Lazare, Elena, 50
Leal, Fernando (letter writer), 133
Leto, Gerónima, 62
letters, la patria and, 108–26; historical background and, 108–10; illness and, 119; letters from children and, 121–22; national holidays and, 119–21; pardons and, 124–25; Spanish immigrants and, 115–16; vagrant boys and, 109
letter subjects: amnesty and, 97, 139; Argentine caudillos and, 2; automobiles, trucks and, 102–3, 141–42; bureaucracy and, 131; divorce and, 92–93; domestic servants, wages and benefits and, 91;

letter subjects (*continued*)
economic matters and, 95, 97;
fascism, workers' benefits and,
91; homeless children and, 93,
137; immigration and, 101; inventions and, 101–4; land auctions
and, 91–92; land reform (emphyteusis) and, 95; literacy, schools
and and, 10, 93–95; mortgages,
foreclosures, evictions and,
96–97; Mother's Day and, 134–35;
nationalism, unity and, 2; needs
of the rural poor, elderly and, 3;
police and, 135, 139; strong
authoritarian executive and, 90;
women, equal rights for and,
98–99; workers' pay and benefits
and, 91, 132
letter-writing as political mechanism,
37–38
Lorenzo, Rosalinda, 60–61
Lucca, Gino, 79–80
Luna, Juan (letter writer), 99–100
Lupini, Marta (letter writer), 119
Lura, Marco (letter writer), 92

Madsen, Douglas, 7
Maduro, Nicolás, 146
Main, María (Fleur Cowles), 4
Mangioni, Elenora de (letter writer),
26–27
Manzi, Homero: "Songs of a Minstrel to
Sra. Eva Perón," 9, 9–10
Marconi, Zulema, 137
María Eva Duarte de Perón Social Aid,
45
Martes, Rita (letter writer), 25
Martínez, Bonita de (letter writer),
118–19
Martínez, Edgardo, 50
Martínez, Osvaldo (letter writer), 97
Martínez, Tomás Eloy, 144

Mende, Raúl, 131
Menem, Carlos Saúl, 145
Mercante, Domingo, 22, 34–35, 42,
44–45, 72
Mercedes-Benz, 102
Milanesio, Natalia, 86
"Milonga descamisada" (tango), 9
Ministerio de Asuntos Técnicos, 68–69
Ministerio de Trabajo y Previsión, 63
Ministry of Technical Subjects, 86,
101–4
Mirabia, Irma (letter writer), 138
Monte, Petrona Ríos, 48
Morelli, Aldo (letter writer), 134
Moreno, Francisco P., 109
Morón, Sara, 137
Mundo Peronista, 89, 105, 144

Nación, La, 70
Naon, Miguel, 60
National Department of Social
Assistance, 32
Navarro, Maryssa, 19, 52, 59–60, 88,
154n41; *Eva Perón*, 5
Neuman, William, 145
New York Times: Eva and, 21; on the
five-year plan, 70

Oscar (letter writer), 29–30
Otey, María Clara de, 53
Ottone, Elvira (letter writer), 97

Pack, George, 87
Page, Joseph A., 6
Paloma, Ramona, 110–11
Pan-American Act of Chapultepec, 22
Paquiano, Sra. (letter writer), 88
Partera, Sara Jessica (letter writer), 29
Patronato de la Infancia, 109
Patronato Español, 116
Patronato Nacional de Menores, 112
Pattinato, Carlos (letter writer), 30

pensions, subsidies: application for, 45–46; Buenos Aires public assistance and, 42; charismatic links with Eva and, 46; Decree No. 15.515, Charitable Subsidies and, 41–42; dependent children and, 51; details of, 43, 50; funding of, 45; an "honest life" and, 43–44; inconsistency, arbitrariness and, 56; legislators and, 56; letters and, 46–51; Mothers' Pension Fund and, 42; Society of Beneficence and, 41, 42; trade unions and, 41–42; widows and, 44

Pérez, Guillermo (letter writer), 90

Perón, Eva Duarte de, 1, 147n4; antibiotics and, 22; "bridge of love" and, 3, 38, 88, 141, 154n41; death of, 89; hogares de tránsito and, 23; illness of, 87–88; immigrant women and, 27–28; inflated titles and, 48; last will and testament of, 88; as madrina, 21; poor children and, 22; radio programs and, 4, 147n10; *razón de mi vida, La,* 4, 21; religiosity of, 5; Society of Beneficence and, 37; tango and, 90; victims of the 1944 earthquake and, 28; welfare state and, 2; women's suffrage and, 22. *See also* Duarte, Eva

Perón, Juan, 1; charismatic populist politics and, 6, 84; death of, 145; Depression, World War II, rural poor and, 14–15; Eva Perón Foundation and, 65; five-year plans and, 2–3; immigrant groups and, 15; laborers and, 6; legitimacy strategies and, 7, 67–68; mass-media campaign of 1946, 68; policy suggestions and, 71; press conference, September 1946, 68–69; press conferences, October 1947, 69–70; on Society of Beneficence, 34; tango and, 9, 29, 148n26

Peronism, 135–36; bureaucratic facilities and, 130; charismatic populist politics and, 3, 146; early years of, 36–37; election of 1952 and, 129; Eva's illness and, 88; feminine side of, 39; inflation and, 140; limits of power and, 131–32, 136–37; loyalty and, 129; presidential powers and, 150n39; women and, 129

Peronist Women's Political Party, 4

Peróns, 5; bank accounts of, 5; biographical accounts of, 3; charisma, letter writing and, 1; destruction of letters of, 8; government-subsidized philanthropies and, 29–31; popular culture and, 7–8, 9; Spiritism and, 5; welfare state and, 3

personalismo, 4

petitions, written, in Spanish America, 13

philanthropies, 149n28

Piramo, Daniela di, 7

Pirán, Belisario Cache (letter writer), 125

Pirelli, Eloisa de (letter writer), 129

Pitone, Florencio (letter writer), 59–60

Plan de Gobierno (Plan Quinquenal): General Confederation of Labor and, 70; hopes of Peronism and, 69; leadership path and, 68; legislative consolidation and, 68; newspapers and, 81; *Perón cumple su Plan de Gobierno,* 82; specific goals and, 68; successes of, 85

Plotkin, Mariano Ben, 59; *Mañana es San Perón,* 6

policy suggestions (letters): agricultural prices and, 76; apartment construction and, 77; charismatic populist politics and, 84; domestic servants, training and certification of, 72–73; immigration, colonization and, 79–80, 82; irrigation systems and, 76; land inheritance and, 81–82; land reform (emphyteusis) and, 71–72, 74; mental health and, 74; quantity of, 84; school construction and, 79; social security and, 80–81; sugar cane prices and, 77–79; teachers' salaries and, 80–81; textile factory and, 76–77; volunteering and, 74–75

Potash, Robert, 6

Prensa, La, 34, 81

presidential histories in Latin America, 1

Provano, José (letter writer), 121

Quilmes, Ronaldo (letter writer), 116

Raíces, Paulina (letter writer), 62

Ramírez, General Pedro, 25

Ramírez, Luis (letter writer), 103

razón de mi vida, La (Perón, Eva), 4, 21

Rega, José López (letter writer), 145

Renzi, Atilio, 58, 130

Resifra, Constanzo (letter writer), 61–62

Reyes, Raimundo (letter writer), 54

Reynals, Noemí (letter writer), 89

Ricardo, Bárbara (petitioner), 60

Rivadavia, Bernardino (letter writer), 71

Rivera, Analía Cuenta de (letter writer), 24

Rivera, Celestina (letter writer), 57–58

Robles, Saturnino, 103–4

Román, Zeno (letter writer), 103

Romero, Aldo (letter writer), 63

Romero, María Clara de (letter writer), 139

Rosas, Juan Manuel de, 2

Rosas, Juan Manuel de, doña Encarnación and, 4, 147n4

Rousseff, Dilma, 145

Saletti, Eduardo (letter writer), 93–94

Salvatore, Ricardo, 2

Sánchez, Petronella, 49

San Martín, Armando Méndez, 26, 30, 32, 35, 45, 56, 105, 130–31

Saone, Santiago (letter writer), 136–37

Sarmiento, Domingo, president, 13

Segundo Plan Quinquenal: charisma and, 86; children and, 104–5; delay of, 85–86; failure and successes of, 105; letter writing and, 86; outstanding issues and, 85–86; wide-ranging responses and, 87. *See also under* inflation

Snow, Peter G., 7

social problems, 14–15, 43; homeless children and, 93, 137; immigration to and within Argentina, 15, 67; la patria letters and, 111; rural poverty and, 11, 37, 144. *See also under* letter subjects

Society of Beneficence, 5, 10–11, 14; adoption and, 25–26; boarding schools and, 26; Boys' Orphanage and, 108; Integral Plan and, 33c; Juan and Eva Perón and, 32; letter files and, 5; Mercante, Domingo and, 44–45; orphan girls and, 109; Peronists and, 35; reform plans and, 32–33; San Martín and, 32–33

Society of Beneficence of Jewish Ladies, 24

"Songs of a Minstrel to Sra. Eva Perón" (Manzi), 9–10

Soto, Andrés (letter writer), 63

Soza, Cipriano (letter writer), 54

Taylor, Julie M., 5; *Eva Perón: Myths of a Woman*, 5–6

Time magazine, 4; Eva and, 21

Union of Workers of Various Professions, 53

Vásquez, Paulino (letter writer), 63

Veinte años perdidos (Gorman), 70–71

Victorio, Juan (letter writer), 26

Weber, Max, 7

welfare organizations, 149n28

women and Peronism, 18; First Argentine Feminine League in Support of Maternity and Children, 134; Jewish women and, 24–25; Women's Advisory Commission and, 36; Women's Hospital for the Insane and, 23; Women's Peronist Party and, 60–61. *See also under* Perón, Eva Duarte de

Yrigoyen, Hipólito, president, 14, 148n3

Zaída, María (letter writer), 136

Zapata, Hernán Costa, 76